Stirring It Up

PAUL MASEK

Copyright 2007 by Paul Masek

www.stirringitup.org

Published by Out of the Box Records, St. Louis, MO

www.outoftheboxrecords.com

Imprimatur
Most Reverend Robert J. Hermann
Auxiliary Bishop of St. Louis

Table of Contents

Dedication
& Mad Props

I dedicate this book to my children – to my favorite twins Audrey and Jacob who recently became teenagers, and to Kyle and Dominic who will be teens before I know it. You are all growing up so fast! I hope that something (even if it is only one thing) in this book will help guide you through the turbulent teenage years. I pray for you every day that you will always stay close to Jesus and that you will come into adulthood relatively unscathed, while learning from any scars. Know that He will always be with you – especially when I cannot be.

Since all the big rock stars (like my friends Adam and Dominic) always get to say all kinds of random stuff and thank lots of people on their albums, and since this is the closest I will ever come (alas!) to being a rock star, I would like to thank Jesus for constantly trying to save me from myself, and my stunning bride Lisa - who does the same while remaining the most beautiful woman I will ever know. And, in no particular order, I want to acknowledge these profound influences on my life – the people who have let me into their hearts and let me share their stories, everyone on the REAP Team, Men's Group for being the brothers I never had, Growlers Pub, fire, whoever invented Diet Coke, coffee, Skittles, and Sugar Babies, Dan who is the man for the challenge of creative titling, Steve for his flawless vocal talents on the CD, Dominic the master at mastering, Larry Boy, my proofreaders who stretched me (especially my dad for contributing his English professorial skills!), the times with the other two stooges, God for creating this world and for lots of fun food like sunflower seeds, Bill Gates so I didn't have to write this book on a typewriter with correction ribbon like I used to write my papers in college, the OYM and CYA, my H.T. family, the inspirational man I affectionately call "Uncle Ray", Bishop Hermann, God's Gang, Catholicism, C.S. Lewis, Donald Miller, The Lost Dogs, Benedictine College, my mom and dad for sacrificing so much for me and buying the cabin in Belle so I can get away, Ray the web guy for stirringitup. org, Pete for helping me to burn the promo CDs, my sisters, the countless teens I have met who inspire me so much, Father John my pastor for being such an amazing priest and confidante, JP II, Benny One-Six, and all who have ever loved me and prayed for me – please don't stop. Ever.

Awe, Fear, a Trigger, and Doubt

My feeling about people in whose conversion I have been allowed to play a part is always mixed with awe and even fear: Such as a boy might feel on first being allowed to fire a rifle. The disproportion between his puny finger on the trigger and the thunder and lightning which follow is alarming. And the seriousness with which the other party takes my words always raises the doubt whether I have taken them seriously enough myself... Think of me as a fellow-patient in the same hospital who, having been admitted a little earlier, could give some advice.

    -- C.S. Lewis (1)

I think of these words of C.S. Lewis often. I know that I am just one guy, and I am more aware than anyone else (besides my God and my wife) what a sinner I am. However, I have learned that my own sin and weakness should never be an excuse that keeps me from sharing what I have learned, especially about my relationship with God. That would be what is called 'false humility', a disease that far too many people – and therefore the world – have been infected by.

My reason for writing this book is simply to encourage you to deepen your own personal relationship with God. I promise to share with you only the things that have really helped me, in the hope that they will help you. I am going to stick to the basics, sharing with you the tools that I believe will help you stay connected to God, whether you are a beginner in this journey or a veteran. Some things may speak to you at this moment in your life, and some "not so much"; but you might want to consider re-reading this book periodically, since your relationship with God (and mine!) is constantly changing and growing, and since different tools will therefore be more helpful than others at different times.

Though I believe that this book will be helpful to anyone who wants to grow in his or her faith, it is written specifically with teenagers in mind. It is for the teenagers I have met and will continue to meet as a youth minister, for those I will never meet but who may happen to pick up this book, and for my own children – two of whom are currently teenagers, and two who will be teenagers soon.

The title of this book comes from a simple analogy that I frequently share with teenagers on Confirmation retreats with the REAP Team (2), the ministry I coordinate in the Archdiocese of St. Louis. The analogy goes like this –

> *In some ways, we are like a glass of milk – we are good, but we have the potential to be more than we already are. The gift of the Holy Spirit is, in some ways, like chocolate syrup. It is poured into our lives when we are baptized, as a free gift from God; but often it just sits there, inactive, at the bottom of the glass. All of*

that power – the power through which the Universe was created – is within each one of us; and yet our life – like the milk – remains unchanged unless the Holy Spirit is stirred up! This 'stirring up' begins when we make a commitment to Jesus, and it continues as we take steps to grow closer to Jesus. And any time we cooperate with God's grace and allow the Holy Spirit to be stirred up in our lives, our lives become sweeter, though not always easier, but more and more full with the certain knowledge of how much God loves us and wants to be with us at all times.

This concept of 'stirring it up' is not a new idea, by the way, as it is referenced in the Bible –

I remind you to stir into flame the gift of God that you have through the imposition of my hands. For God did not give us a spirit of cowardice but rather of power and love and self-control. (3)

For the sake of my analogy, I think it would be fair to paraphrase this Scripture passage –

I remind you to stir up the Holy Spirit in your life, so that your life may be so much more than boring white milk – rather, that it will become rich, flavorful chocolate milk! For God wants us to experience the power of His Spirit so that we will not be afraid, but rather be full of power and love and self-control! (4)

Again, it is my hope and my prayer that each chapter of this book will give you practical tips for growing closer to Jesus and therefore will result in the Holy Spirit being more stirred up in your life.

Finally, I want to acknowledge that I am indebted to countless saints, living on Earth and in Heaven, for any wisdom in this book. If this book contained only my wisdom, it would be way shorter and far less wise than it is!

Pleasure to Angels

John was driving down the street in a sweat because he was running late to a very important meeting and couldn't find a parking place. Looking up toward heaven, he said, "Lord, help me. If you find me a parking place, I will not only go to church every Sunday for the rest of my life, but I will even give up beer." Just then, a parking place miraculously appeared! John then looked up again to heaven and said, "Never mind, Lord. I found one."

I love that story because it's funny and because it strikes me as true. I have to admit that I have prayed that way before. I have bargained with God, and then I've gone back on my end of the deal. I have had my prayers answered, and then I've forgotten to thank God. I'll honestly admit that I am not an expert at praying; I wish that I prayed more and that I knew how to pray better. For those reasons, it is humbling and feels weird to be writing a chapter on prayer; lucky for you, though, I am going to share some wisdom that goes way beyond my own sphere of knowledge.

When I am asked to speak to a group of teenagers on prayer, I usually ask them to raise their hands if they have ever prayed. And, guess what – almost everyone raises their hand! Chances are that you have prayed at some point in your life, either for yourself or for someone else. You know, as I do, that there are times when we need help from someone bigger than ourselves, times when we are grateful for how we have been blessed, and times when loved ones need help that we simply cannot give them. Since deep down in our hearts we believe that God loves us and wants to help us out, we pray.

Prayer is awesome. It warms the heart of God; God loves it when we pray. He loves us more than we could possibly imagine, He is always available to us, and He wants to spend time with us. That, very simply, is what prayer is about – spending time with God. Even though most people I know would admit that they pray sometimes, most of those same people would confess that they probably could pray more or pray better. If you have ever felt that way, then this chapter is for you.

The purpose of this chapter is to give you some practical advice on how to strengthen and deepen your prayer life because prayer is the best and most important way to stay connected to God and keep the Holy Spirit stirred up in our lives. Not only that, but prayer offers us a sense of peace and security here on Earth, as well as a connection with God that can last forever.

Motivation

One of my problems for the longest time was that I really wasn't very motivated to pray. Have you ever felt that way? I knew that praying was a good thing and all, but it just wasn't nearly as interesting as what I could find on TV or surfing the web. I meant no disrespect to God, but I used to find prayer kind of boring and felt too busy with other things to pray. So what I did (and it really worked!) was that I simply asked God to motivate me to pray. And, since God knows me better than anyone else does, He eventually got my attention and gave me the motivation I needed. I will not get into all of the details of how God motivated me right now; but if you listen to the track entitled "Deer Hunting with God" on the CD that goes with this book, you'll find out what happened. So my advice, if you lack motivation to pray, is simply this: spend some time every day asking God to motivate you to pray. Then pay close attention, because God will do something to motivate you. He might even surprise you (as He surprised me) by what He does.

A final thought on motivation, which has helped me a great deal as I have reflected on it, comes from Fr. Segundo Galilea who writes "...the ultimate, persistent motivation for prayer and its solid foundation is the conviction that God loves us and offers us the gift of liberating friendship." (5) What this wise priest is saying is that I should pray not because I will feel guilty if I don't, but because prayer is a response to God's incredible love and because prayer is the best way for me to deepen my friendship with God, who has already chosen to be my best friend. I like that.

Temptation

My pastor once told me that he rarely speaks about the devil from the pulpit because he feels like he never has enough time to talk about the Lord! If you have ever been on a retreat with me or heard me do public speaking, you will know that I tend to agree with him; I rarely talk about the devil, either. But since we are now exploring ways to enhance our prayer lives, it is important to be honest about the influence of the evil one. I wish I could remember who said it (so I could give them credit in my footnotes), but is has been said that "the greatest temptation of the devil upon good people (like you and me) is that the devil tempts us to delay, neglect, or shorten our prayer time." How about you? Have you ever been tempted to delay, neglect, or shorten your prayer time? I've experienced this temptation countless times - and far too many times I have given in to that temptation.

It is a fact that the evil one is real, and he hates you. He hates me. He hates the fact that you are reading this book, and he hates it when we pray. Knowing this, it really helps me to think about prayer as going to battle for God, for my soul, and for the souls of those I love. Maybe I love this war imagery because I'm a guy and such a huge fan of epic war movies like *The Lord of the Rings, Braveheart, Gladiator, Band of Brothers,* and *Saving Private Ryan.* But even if you are not a fan of fighting, it is a fact that there is a constant battle raging every day for your soul. The good news is that to be a winner all we need to do is to unite ourselves with Jesus, who has conquered the devil through His death and resurrection. And we totally unite ourselves to His victory when we pray. I don't know about you, but that gets me totally fired up to pray! I don't want the evil one to beat me up; I want to stand strong and victorious – even if I get a little bloodied and bruised - in this raging battle.

Regarding this battle we're in, I will never forget the story my friend Jeff told me after going on a retreat led by some religious men. They actually compared the Rosary to a gun (yes, you can actually hold it that way!) and the prayer beads as bullets to shoot down the evil one. That is a pretty cool analogy. And if you know anything about the enemy's hatred of Mary and the Rosary, you have to admit that the analogy is not too far off.

Don't let temptation bother you too much, though, OK? It is perfectly normal. Everyone gets tempted. Jesus was tempted not only when He prayed

(6), but throughout His entire life (7). Another very powerful thought is just to know that if you are being tempted by the devil to delay, neglect, or shorten your own prayer, that is a compliment; the devil would not be tempting you if you were not a real threat to his activity in your life and in your world. Whenever you are tempted to be a wimp about praying, then pray a little bit more! Consider what the great St. John Chrysostom said -

> *Prayer well made gives much pleasure to angels, and therefore it is much assisted by them; it gives great displeasure to the devils, and therefore is much persecuted and disturbed by them. (8)*

A final word about temptation – our Catholic tradition teaches that temptation actually comes from three sources: the world, the flesh, and the devil. The world is everything in our society that is opposed to or disinterested in God, including the influences of the media and peer pressure. The flesh is our own human weaknesses in our fallen nature, including laziness and selfishness. And the devil is a punk who is just completely annoying. Never forget that God is more powerful than any of these influences. We just need to tap into His power - which we do when we pray - in order to resist the temptations that constantly come our way to keep us from praying.

Praying All Day Long

An excellent way to pray is to offer the entire day, every day, as a prayer to God. We can do this by simply trying, all day long, to be aware of God's presence in our lives. We can give God permission to be with us and work through us. We can stay in regular communication with Him all day by talking to Him whenever we think of Him, thanking Him whenever we are grateful, praying for others when we think of them, asking Him for what we need, and filling our day with prayers from our heart. Prayers like this do not need to be long; I happen to be a fan of prayers that are short, sweet, and to-the-point. This kind of ongoing prayer takes a lot of practice, but I am sure that God is thrilled with any efforts we make. If we continually try to pray all day long, it can become a habit and therefore much easier to do. Prayer like this brings untold amounts of peace and joy, because we are consistently connecting with God. Our entire lives can become a prayer to God! The great spiritual writer Brother Lawrence put it like this:

> *There is not in the world a kind of life more sweet and delightful, than that of a continual conversation with God. Those only can comprehend it who practice and experience it. (9)*

To explore this concept more fully, you might want to check out www.practicegodspresence.com, which has some great resources, including some printable mini-books. I started browsing this site while writing this book, and I could have spent hours reading and printing out the resources I found. It is a site that I have bookmarked, and I plan on going back to it on a regular basis to inspire and encourage me in my attempts to pray all day long.

Personal Prayer Time

Another excellent way to pray is to develop a daily personal prayer time. This is simply finding some way of spending some quality time alone every day with God. Exactly what you do during your personal prayer time is between you and God and is a very personal thing; that is why it is called *personal* prayer time. Know, though, that the possibilities are endless - including reading the Bible, praying the Rosary, Adoration, having a conversation with God from your heart, praying more traditional prayers like the Lord's Prayer or Hail Mary, listening to inspirational music, simply being quiet, or some combination of these or other things. What matters is that you do what works for you and helps you to connect with God. And what works for you may change from day to day and may develop over time. How much time you spend in personal prayer time is up to you, too; if you have never taken personal prayer time before now, I encourage you to start small with a realistic amount of time. Maybe five minutes in the morning, maybe five minutes at night. I have found that the more time I spend in personal prayer time, the more time I want to spend in personal prayer time.

As you try to develop a personal prayer time, I encourage you to think about what fits your lifestyle and that you consider asking God for His input. That's what I did, and I am so glad that I did. Several years ago, I was very frustrated. I had been struggling for way too long with a very inconsistent personal prayer life and even though I was a full-time youth minister, I knew that my own personal prayer life was pretty weak. I had not been praying well and wasn't even sure how and when to pray. Add to that the fact that I had just gotten into trouble with my doctor for being in poor physical shape and living what he called a 'sedentary lifestyle.' Basically, that means that I had become physically lazy (in addition to my spiritual laziness), and so he told me I needed to find a way to exercise. But how could I fit an exercise routine and personal prayer time into my busy schedule? I mean, I thought I was the busiest person I knew! Unsure what to do, I finally just cried out to God, asking Him what he wanted me to do. And, guess what? He spoke to my heart. "Pray while you exercise; kill two birds with one stone." God is so wise; I decided to follow His advice, and to this day I still do. Every day I spend my personal prayer time with God while either walking on the treadmill or walking outdoors. This totally works for me with my lifestyle and helps me to stay both physically and spiritually fit. I really like to take my personal prayer time in the morning – even though I am not a 'morning person' – because when I do, it sets the tone and helps to prepare my heart for what each day will bring.

Keep in mind, though, that what works for me may not work for you. Maybe you are a night owl and the best quality time you can give to God is at night. Think about it, and pray about it. Then, start experimenting with different ways and times to have a personal prayer time. Take it from me; it is an experiment worth conducting. I am convinced that if you make personal prayer time a part of your daily routine, it will change your life for the better. It has done so for me. And any time we grow closer to God, it enhances our quality of life.

Both Are Essential

I am convinced both of these ways of praying – praying all day long and having personal prayer time - are essential to developing the best relationship with

God that we can possibly have. One without the other would be like Macaroni without Cheese, Itchy without Scratchy, Batman without Robin, Mario without Luigi, Jack without Jill, Popeye without Olive Oyl, Wayne without Garth, Homer without Marge, Paul without Lisa, Abbott without Costello (that was for my old-school friends) or Frodo without Sam! I hope you get the idea. One without the other is simply incomprehensible and reeks of incompleteness. A friend of mine, a 17 year old named Nathan, found the balance of incorporating both praying all day and personal prayer time into his life. He put it like this –

> *My whole day is one big prayer. I wake up in the morning and light a candle before I head upstairs for breakfast, asking God to give me the strength to live that day for Him. I listen to Christian music on the way to school and praise Him through my voice. While at school I try to show others the light of Christ within me; and I end the day the same way that I started it, by lighting a candle and giving thanks and praise to the Lord. A big resource that I use, apart from my voice, is my group of friends. Most us of are very religious people who belong to various youth groups around St. Louis. We always talk to one another, reminding each other to pray about decisions that we have to make and thanking God when things go our way.*

How to Pray

I hope you find it comforting, as I certainly do, that if you don't know how to pray, then you are just like the disciples of Jesus. In the New Testament, they asked Jesus, "Lord, teach us how to pray." (10) They knew they needed help. And because they asked, Jesus gave them, and all of us, the Lord's Prayer! (11) I sure am glad they asked, because I have prayed the Lord's Prayer thousands of times in my life. I believe that if Jesus gave them something so specific when they asked for advice, He will do the same for you. Ask him, "Lord, teach me to pray. How do you want me to pray?" And then listen to Him; He will speak to your heart.

Not only can God teach us directly how to pray, but He can also teach us through other people. I encourage you to ask people you trust for advice on how to pray better; especially ask those people whose spirituality you admire and whose personalities and lifestyles are similar to yours. There is wisdom all around us if we are willing to seek it out. Thousands of books have been written on prayer, and the Church offers us tons of wisdom on how to pray through her teachings, homilies, spiritual direction, and the writings of the saints. In other words, though prayer is very personal, we don't have to reinvent the wheel – there are experts on prayer that we can learn a lot from. And, if you spend a lot of time in the online world, there are even great prayer resources on the Internet. (12)

I urge you to keep in mind that just because someone else has found a way to pray that works for them, that it does not necessarily mean that God wants you to pray that way. However, don't fall into the trap of placing limits on God. Never assume that a style or method of prayer is not for you without giving it a fair chance; that would be like deciding you don't want one of your Christmas gifts without first unwrapping it!

Where to Pray

We can pray anywhere, of course, because God is everywhere. In the song "Pray Where You Are" by a band called *The Lost Dogs*, the lyrics say, "in the fields and in the factories, there's no limits, rules or boundaries – at work or school or driving in your car, pray where you are." (13) I like that. And though it is true that we can pray anywhere at any time, some people have discovered that they have favorite places to pray. It might be that you feel closest to God on the beach or in the mountains and that you have had your best prayer time there; but most of us don't go to the mountains or the beach every day (unless you have a great imagination or live somewhere other than the Midwest)! I recently read a book by a priest who told me that one of his favorite places to pray is in the tree stand during deer season. (14) I can relate to him since I love to pray in the woods when hunting or just walking around. So we can pray anywhere, but I want to encourage you to think about a place that you have daily access to that you can set aside for your daily prayer time. Possible places that might work could include your bedroom, backyard, a park, where you work out, in the shower, in a chapel, on the bus, in the car, or at some other location. It may sound scandalous, but I even know a teenage guy who admitted to me that his best prayer time is when he goes to the bathroom. It works for him because it's something he does every day, and it's certainly a time that he is alone with God! In my opinion, the most important thing about a location for daily prayer time is that it be a place with easy access that is relatively free from distractions.

Creating a Mood

Since most of us Catholics really appreciate rituals and symbols, setting a mood for your prayer time can be helpful. Some people turn off the lights in their room and light a candle when they pray – if you do this, just don't be like my friend Shaun who left the candle lit and started a fire in his house! But, if you are cautious, a candle is a powerful symbol that helps us focus and reminds us of the light of Christ. Some people hold a cross or a crucifix when they pray; or they look at a statue or picture of Jesus, Mary, or a favorite saint. Some people dim their lights; some prefer to kneel or sit down. Some prefer background music, and some prefer total silence. The symbols you use or what you do to create the mood might be very personal, and there are many creative options. Personally, I almost always drink coffee when I pray, since coffee and conversation go together for me. And since I try to take my personal prayer time early in the morning, the caffeine helps me to wake up!

Distractions

Have you ever tried to pray and found yourself totally distracted by a million other things? This is such a huge problem for me – I am so often and so easily distracted - that sometimes I wonder if I might be undiagnosed ADD! I wonder if the chicken came first or if it was the egg? I like tacos, too. You see what I mean?

Focus...well, I do have just a couple of suggestions for dealing with distractions that I have found to be helpful. First of all, I keep a notepad and a pen in the place where I take my personal prayer time. Then, if a thought comes into my mind about something that I need to remember while I'm praying, I write it down and then deal with it later. Second, I have learned to pray about the distraction. Maybe God has allowed that thought or idea to cross my mind because that person or situation needs my prayers. I try not to automatically push away distractions, not only since that is hard to do, but also because I want to be open to the possibility that my distraction might be a gift from God or a way that the Holy Spirit is trying to get my attention.   In this regard, St. Therese said –

> I have many distractions, but as soon as I am aware of them, I pray for those people the thought of whom is diverting my attention. In this way, they reap the benefit of my distractions. (15)

In other words, if you try talking to God about what is distracting you, then conversation with God continues; and then the distraction is not really a distraction. Sweet!

More Random Thoughts on Prayer in No Particular Order

In my life, I have heard countless tips on how to pray better. So now I am going to get very random and shoot out some additional ideas and thoughts I have heard about, read about, or tried. If any of these sound intriguing and if you think they might enhance your prayer life, consider them a gift. If any of them sound lame or bore you, just forget about them. It won't hurt my feelings. But if your prayer life ever gets stale, you might want to consider coming back to these thoughts.

- Pray Naked – this band I love called *The 77s* released a CD called *Pray Naked* a few years ago; some Christian bookstores wouldn't carry it because of the title – it was just a little too scandalous. However, all they were trying to say is that when we pray we should come as we are, without our masks, and be willing to be completely open and transparent with God – since He knows us and loves us as we are. And we don't need to always use formal prayers and churchy language with God; it is enough just to speak from the heart. You can even use slang with God, if that is how you speak to your friends, since God is your homey, true dat!
- Be Emotional – God is the creator of all emotions, so don't be afraid to let your emotions out in prayer. It is 100% OK to laugh, cry, express anger, rejoice, sing, and shout when you pray. You can pray loudly, or softly. Whatever best expresses how you feel. I think God really appreciates our emotional honesty.
- Be Traditional – prayers written by others are awesome, and they sometimes express what we could not express quite so well all by ourselves. Don't neglect the prayers you learned as a child – the Act of Contrition, Our Father, Hail Mary, Glory Be, Rosary, etc. There are great prayer books, written prayers, and other holy writings that will deepen your prayer life if you use them.
- Use a Journal – for some people I know, this is their favorite way to pray. A journal can be like a diary about your relationship with God. You can

write down your prayers and thoughts and feelings, write Him letters, and write your petitions. If you do this, it can be a cool record of your spiritual journey that you can periodically go back to and see how you have grown and how your prayers have been answered. You can create your own journal out of a spiral notebook, and you can even buy prayer journals at Christian bookstores; some of them give you an inspirational thought or Bible verse that can be a focal point of your journaling time.

- Music – whether you play music, listen to music, or like to sing, there is something very spiritual about music – so use it any way that you can to help enhance your prayer life. Lyrics of Christian (and even some secular) music can help us to pray. I have a playlist on my IPod of Christian music that lifts my heart to God. I know musicians who just pick up their guitar and sing and play to God. Lots of people sing in the shower; why not sing out some praise to God the next time you shower – which we all hope will be soon! As St. Augustine said, "Singing is praying twice." (16)
- Find a prompter – something that reminds you to pray. A guy I know named Chris told me that for him, it is McDonald's – every time he sees a McDonald's he prays. So when he is driving around, he prays a lot since those pesky restaurants are everywhere. A 2nd grader I knew once heard this idea about having a prompter, so she decided to pray every time the car she was in stopped at a red light; the red light reminded her of the Blood of Jesus. Some folks pray every time they see an emergency vehicle or hear a siren. Some people pray when they brush their teeth. If this thought sounds intriguing, ask God to give you a prompter.
- Mix it up – though I think it is important to find ways and methods of prayer that work for you, there is always more to learn. I encourage you to keep an open heart about new ways of praying. We should never stop learning about prayer, and we should never stop trying to pray.

Finally, I want to remind you that for any relationship to be a good one, it is critical that we not only talk, but that we also become good listeners. This next chapter is going to explore what it means to listen to God and how important this is for our lives.

Shut Up!

(praying for death and black shoes)

There is an amazing story that I have heard on several occasions. Two men were walking down a busy city street, and one said to another, "Do you hear that cricket chirping?" His friend thought he was crazy - how could anyone hear a cricket chirping amidst the noises of the city - cars, buses, horns, voices, etc. The first man, however, walked over to a nearby stone, gently lifted it, and sure enough – there was a cricket. His friend asked him, "How could you possibly have heard that cricket in the midst of all this other noise?" He replied, "Watch this." He took a coin from his pocket, threw it up in the air; and when it hit the sidewalk, everyone within several feet stopped to look for it. At this, the first man replied, "People hear what they want to hear." I believe with all of my heart that each and every one of us can hear God if we want to.

There is an inspiring passage in the Bible in 1 Kings, Chapter 19 where this prophet named Elijah was struggling so much that he wanted to die; he even prayed for death! After this prayer, several interesting things happened to him, including an encounter with an angel, eating some food, and doing some traveling. However, God really wanted to speak to him, so God asked him to stand on a mountain. Then he told Elijah that He would be passing by. Some awesome things happened – a strong wind so powerful that it crushed rocks, an earthquake, and a fire. But, for Elijah, God's voice was not heard in any of this stuff. What happened after all of those dramatic events is that there was a "tiny whispering sound". And it was in that whisper that Elijah heard God.

There is an awesome woman I know named Sister Carol, who has an incredible job. She is a vocation director, which means that she gets to help people learn to listen to God and help them to discern (which just means 'prayerfully figure out') what God is calling them to do with their lives. She has taught me a lot of things, but one of the most memorable lessons she has ever taught me is that in order to figure out God's plan for our lives, we need to, "Shut Up!" (17) I like that. It is always cool when a religious sister tells you to shut up, and I have found it to be true and necessary.

There is a time in the life of my daughter that I will never forget. When Audrey was in preschool, she really needed some black shoes for a wedding that she was going to be in. As she and my wife Lisa shopped, they simply could not find anything in Audrey's size that we could afford. Frustrated, Lisa stopped outside of a shoe store, on a sidewalk, and prayed with Audrey, "Jesus, if you could help us to find some shoes for Audrey, that would be great." As soon as this prayer ended, Audrey looked into her mother's eyes and confidently said, "He said yes." Sure enough, they found just the right shoes in the very next store!

If you are like me, you may not have Audrey's childlike faith, and you may have trouble shutting up when you pray. It may also be difficult for you to hear that quiet whispering voice of God, perhaps because there is so much noise all around you or perhaps you are simply not tuned in to God. Perhaps you've even wondered if God still speaks to His people. Maybe you believe that

God does still speak to some people, but only to those really special and holy people like Biblical figures, saints, and church leaders. Maybe you don't really believe, deep down in your heart, that God cares enough to speak to you. If you have ever felt any of these things, you are not alone. I have, too. But, I have great news for you. God still does want to speak to us; we just need to listen.

As the first story in this chapter highlights, a big part of the reason that so few of us in today's world can hear God is that we live in such a busy and noisy world. There is always so much to do, and there seems to be constant noise everywhere and at all times – radio, conversations, video games, music, television, IPods, computers. And constant activities fill most of our lives. When we hop into our cars to go somewhere, most of us immediately turn on the radio or pop in a CD. Don't worry; I am not saying that these things are always bad. My goal in life is definitely not to be your travel agent for your next guilt trip (I think we've all been on enough of those already)! I readily admit that these noises constantly surround me, too - and they can be good and fun when used appropriately. However, as you certainly know, they can also consume our time so much that we are seldom at rest and rarely silent. So, I have a challenge for you (and for myself) - I want to encourage us to try to spend at least some time in complete and total silence, in the presence of God, every day for the rest of our lives. It may be just those couple of minutes in bed before falling asleep. If we could do this, I am confident it would settle our souls and give God the opportunity to speak to our hearts.

If listening to God is something that you are willing to try, please know this - even when we try our hardest to listen, there are times when God won't say anything, and this can feel mighty weird. Even on a very human level I have found this to be true. Early on in any relationship with anyone I have ever known, silence can be very awkward. But don't worry about it a bit if God seems to be silent with you. Just enjoy being in His presence! Take it from someone who has been in love (and who is still madly in love!) - when you love anyone, it is not always all about the words that you say. Sometimes it is enough just to be quiet in the presence of someone that you care deeply about. Early in my relationship with my wife Lisa, we seemed to talk to each other constantly because we were getting to know one another and were uncomfortable with too much silence. But now that we know one another better, sometimes we just love to sit and BE with each other. God has known you your whole life (even if you haven't known Him very well), and He may just want to BE with you and teach you how to just be quiet and BE with Him. There is a great Bible verse about this where God says, "Be still and know that I am God." (18)

That being said, there are two main reasons why I think we should try to listen to God and give Him the chance to speak to our hearts. The first reason is that God is really smart! God is way smarter than you, and way way smarter than me. The theological term for this is 'omniscient'; that means that God knows everything. No human is that smart! I need more smarts because, quite honestly, I often feel kind of dumb and clueless about my life, and so listening to God will make me less dumber than I am - which I really need, as you can probably tell from this sentence. The second reason I think it is important to listen to God is because He is my Creator, and the creator of anything knows best how it works and how it operates. Take my car, for example - not literally, of course, because I need it to get around. To illustrate the point, though, I want to tell you about my car. My Corolla was made by the Toyota Corporation, and so naturally they know how it operates best, how to take care of it, and how to get the most out of it. To help me out, the dealer even gave me an owner's manual when I bought the car. Similarly, God, my Creator, can advise me on how to best operate my life, how to take care of myself, and how to live life to the fullest. God has graciously given an owner's manual to us for our lives, and I have devoted an entire chapter of this book to that - the very next chapter, by the way.

Here is the deal. If we listen to God, and if we are willing to cooperate with what God speaks to our hearts, we can gradually uncover His plan for our lives. Yes, it is true. We can discover God's vision for our lives, and God's vision for our lives is extremely important to know! It is far better than our own vision for our lives could ever be and will really make a difference in this world, as you will discover in a later chapter of this book called "Jon and Amber's Keg Party". The title of that chapter, and what is contains, are so intriguing that I wouldn't blame you one bit if you just stopped right here, put a bookmark on this page, and went straight to that chapter right now.

You see, God cares very deeply about each one of us, in a very personal way - especially about the really important things in our lives: the kind of person we are, the kind of person we will become, our relationships with others, our happiness, and our future. The problem is this – though most people would readily admit that God wants the best for us in all of these areas, most of us live as if we know better than God! Most people, even those of us who profess a belief in God, will choose a dating partner, a college, a career, a marriage partner, a home, and how to spend our money – and then will ask for God's blessing on those things. In my experience, though, very few of us ask God first about such things. How many of us have really asked God questions like these –

> Who do you want me to be friends with, God?
> Should I date that person, God?
> Where should I go to school, God?
> How should I spend my free time, God?
> How should I spend my money, God?
> Where do you want me to live, God?
> Should I marry this person, God?
> What do you want me to do with my life, God?

Even if you have never asked God about such things, it is never too late to start. But hold on tight! Because life with God is an adventure, and He might lead you to some very interesting, challenging, uncomfortable, and even dangerous places. Don't worry, though. He will be with you.

While it is critically important to ask for God's wisdom about these very important facets of our lives, asking will never do us any good at all unless we listen to God's response!

So now that I have shared with you WHY it is so important to listen to God, I want to give you some practical tips on HOW to listen to God. The good news is that there are lots of ways to listen to God – and I am not going to pretend that I know exactly how God is going to speak to you – that is a very private matter between you and God. However, I can offer you some advice because there are some very trustworthy ways that God has, throughout history, spoken to His people.

Since the Bible is God's Word, it is the best place to start. Obviously, right now you are reading my words. When you read the Bible, you will be reading God's words to you. It is a love letter from God to you. It is so important that I have devoted the entire next chapter (called "Ugly Emily") to it – and I hope that chapter will help you to approach God's Word with faith and love. A very famous Catholic saint, before He became a saint, had a life-changing experience with the Bible. Here is Augustine, who later became St. Augustine, telling his story kind of in his own words for you. I say kind of, because I have translated his story (from a book he wrote called *Confessions*) into more modern English for you so that it might be easier for you to understand -

> *I felt so terrible about all of the bad choices I had made in my life that I was crying bitterly. Suddenly, I heard the voice of a young child next door singing, "Pick it up, read it; pick it up, read it." I stopped crying right away, and wondered about this, until I just knew in my heart that God was speaking to me. He was telling me to open the Bible and read the first thing I found. I did. And here is what I read "let us conduct ourselves properly as in the day, not in orgies and drunkenness, not in promiscuity and licentiousness, not in rivalry and jealousy. But put on the Lord Jesus Christ, and make no provision for the desires of the flesh." That was it. I read no more. Immediately, I knew for sure that God was real. He had just spoken to my heart, and all doubt was gone. (19)*

That, my friends, is the power of the Bible. God can speak through it in ways that can transform a really big sinner into a really big saint! Check it out and see what might happen to you.

Another great way that God speaks to us, His people, is through the Church. Those of us who are Catholic believe that the Church is a gift from God, which not only helps us to interpret the Bible properly, but which also can be a excellent guide for us in matters of faith and morals. There are great answers to many of life's most important questions available to us through the wisdom of the Church. Check out *The Catechism of the Catholic Church* (20) and just browse through its "Table of Contents" some time. You'll see what I mean. This wisdom of the Church can be imparted to us in a wide variety of ways – Church documents, teachings of the Popes and Bishops, writings of the saints and other holy people, religious textbooks, inspired preaching and teaching, religion classes, priests, religious brothers and sisters, youth ministers, and teachers – just to name a few. If we ask the right people, there are always answers available to us when we have questions.

God also speaks to us, quite simply, through our thought life – that is, through our imagination. When St. Joan of Arc was on trial for being a heretic, her judges said, "You say God speaks to you-but it's only your imagination." To this, she calmly replied, "...and how else would God speak to me but through my imagination?" (21)

There are countless other ways that God might choose to speak to us – and one of the biggest is through people who really love us. Our parents and our really good friends are a great source of wisdom for our lives because they want what is best for us, even when we can get confused as to what is really best for us. Other ways God speaks to us include things as simple as the beauty of creation (which reflects God's love and power), Christian music, a song on the radio, a hymn at church, a newspaper article, a blog, an email from a friend, a stranger's smile, a little child – I could go on and on. The ways that God speaks to us are too many to mention here; and even if I tried to list them all, I would certainly fail, since God is so creative and varied in the ways He tries to get our attention.

Before I end this chapter, I need to say a few very important words about discernment. (22) As I said earlier, discernment simply means 'prayerfully figuring out' what God wants of us. Before acting upon what we believe God has said to us in our prayer time, especially about really big things in our lives, we need to make sure that it is really God speaking to us. None of us is perfect; and therefore we are all capable of self-deception, thinking that our thoughts are God's thoughts, being innocently misguided, and even being led astray by the powers of evil. I recently read a quote from someone who said that the church (meaning us – God's people) has given God a bad name. Sad, but certainly true! Countless people who have claimed to be following God's voice have brought untold pain and tragedy to our world. Just two examples are terrorists who have destroyed innocent human life (while really believing that they are doing God's will) and church leaders who have proclaimed messages of hate and intolerance. I have even known people who, quite innocently, thought that they heard God speaking to them and later found out that they were wrong. To help to safeguard us against these dangers of not hearing God properly, God has blessed us with several safeguards to help us to discern the voice of God from other voices (the world, our own desires, and the devil). First of all, God would never ask us to do anything inconsistent with what is taught in the Bible, especially Jesus' divine proclamation to love God and other people. And, as I mentioned earlier, we also have the guidance of the Church and church leaders to keep us on the right path. For the big things in life, before immediately following what we perceive to be God's voice, we should always run those ideas past the people who love us well – our parents, our good friends, and even a trusted spiritual guide like a pastor, youth minister, or other person of mature faith. Even though we might be striving to listen to God, we are not the final authority – we need wisdom and guidance to properly discern His voice. Don't forget that, OK?

Finally, I would like to close this chapter with this simple reminder – keep listening! If nothing else, you will certainly hear God telling you how much He loves you. And He does. More than you will ever know.

> *I always begin my prayer in silence, for it is in the silence of the heart that God speaks.*
> *--Mother Teresa (23)*

> *My sheep hear my voice; I know them, and they follow me.*
> *--Jesus (24)*

Ugly Emily

Emily thought she was an ugly teenager. She was going through an especially difficult time in her life because everything was changing. She didn't like her hair, her face, her teeth, or the shape of her body. She didn't think her personality was all that great either. The boys in her class seemed much more interested in talking to and hanging out with the "prettier" girls than with her. Even though Emily's parents really loved her and constantly reminded her of her beauty, she didn't believe it. The world and her friends had convinced her otherwise. Yes, Emily thought she was ugly.

Emily's mom could tell that something was wrong and was unsure what more she could do to help her struggling daughter. In a moment of inspiration, she wrote some words on a slip of paper, which she taped onto Emily's mirror. Emily saw the words but shrugged them off, thinking, "There goes mom again!" Even so, Emily didn't take the paper off of her mirror. She kept it there and continued to read those words each day, for several days, which turned into several months, which became several years. As time passed and she read those words every time she looked in the mirror, they started to sink in; Emily started to believe them. Those words eventually took root, and she is now utterly convinced that those words are absolutely true. Here are the words Emily's mom wrote down for her - "You are made in the image and likeness of God and you are good." You see, those words were not only her mother's words - they were also God's message to Emily, based upon a passage in the Bible. (25) The truth that changed Emily's life and convinced her of her beauty was God's truth!

I love Emily's story because it reminds me how powerful the Bible is, and that is something I can sometimes forget.

There is this great joke that I really hate; I'll tell you why I hate it after I tell you the joke. Here it is –

> *Three people – a Pentecostal, a Baptist, and a Catholic - were discussing the passage from the Bible where Jesus says, "You will know the truth, and the truth will set you free." The Pentecostal said, "Oh, yeah, that passage is somewhere in the Gospel of John, in chapter 8, I do believe." The Baptist said, "To be precise, that passage is in the Gospel of John, Chapter 8, verse 32." And the Catholic responded, "What page is that on?"*

Someone once told me that a joke isn't really funny unless it contains some truth, and that is why I really hate that great joke! Christians in other churches generally know their Bibles quite well, but sadly most of us Catholics are often unfamiliar with our Bibles and lack a deep appreciation of God's Word. But the good news is that it doesn't have to be that way.

I want to be completely honest with you. When I was a young teenager, I wasn't very interested in reading the Bible. Oh, I knew deep down in my heart it was a good book – THE Good Book, as a matter of fact! And I knew that it contained some great stories like the Christmas story, Jonah and the whale,

Noah's ark, the 10 commandments, Jesus' resurrection, and some other pretty mind-blowing miracles. The miracle that inspired me the most was when Jesus turned water into wine at a wedding reception. Even so, I still felt like the Bible was mostly a bunch of big religious words, outdated rules, and restrictive regulations; and that's just not a party waiting to happen when you're trying really hard to be a hip and trendy teenager. So, what changed for me?

What changed, believe it or not, was not the Bible; what changed was my attitude toward the Bible. Here is how that attitude changed. When I was in college, I met some friends who didn't wear masks – they were not only some of the most amazing people and truest friends I had ever met up to that point, but they were deeply committed to Jesus Christ as their best friend. Through a series of events that would take too long to explain here, these friends showed me (through their actions and their words) who Jesus is. Through the faithful influence of these awesome people, Jesus gradually became my best friend, and I eventually decided that I would be better off asking Him to take charge of my life - since I was doing a pretty crummy job as lord of my own life. In a nutshell, that's what happened! Having Jesus in my life is what changed my attitude toward the Bible; and as I have tried to get to know Him better, the Bible has proven to be the best and most trustworthy source of information about Him.

I hope that you are interested in getting to know Jesus better. I can tell you with absolute confidence that getting to know Him better is the best decision I ever made in my life. And here's the deal. As you certainly know, a big part of getting to know someone is to listen to them or read their words, right? Think about it. We get to know our friends through conversation, whether in person, on the phone, or online. We can also get to know them by reading their emails, letters, and online journals. It may sound kind of crazy; but what if you decided today to start looking at the Bible as God's website, blog, Facebook, or MySpace page? Seriously! If you knew for real that the Creator of the Universe had a place like that online where you could find out His thoughts, get advice from Him, and learn about His plan for your life, wouldn't you at least check it out? I would, without hesitation. The honest to God truth is that the Bible is exactly that kind of place - and you can even read it online, if you prefer! (26) It is a place where you can really get to know the one who loves you more than you will ever know.

A big reason that I read the Bible is because of what this guy named Jerry once said to me. Actually, his name is St. Jerome, but I love calling saints by their nicknames, since they are real people just like you and me. Anyway, Jerry once said this, "Ignorance of the Scriptures is ignorance of Christ." (27) Whoa! Dude! I don't know about you, but that is one thing I don't want to be – ignorant of Jesus Christ! He is my best friend, and I want to know as much as possible about Him. As I've said, one of the best ways to know Him is through the Bible, especially the Gospels, which are four different versions of His life and His teachings.

I want to share with you some really practical tips that might help you with your Bible reading; they certainly have helped me. Here they are, in no particular order –

- If you really have no desire to read the Bible, ask God to give you that desire. I think God would really dig it if you would ask Him to increase your desire to read His Word.
- Pick it up. Sorry to insult your intelligence, but far too many people never pick up their Bible. It can help to put your Bible in a place where it will look at you and remind you on a regular basis to pick it up. Consider placing your Bible wherever you normally pray, or somewhere you visit every day - on your nightstand, or in your underwear drawer, or by your toothbrush – hey, whatever works!
- Ask the Holy Spirit to inspire you when you read it; that is something the Holy Spirit just loves to do!
- Read it when you're bored. Come on, you know you get bored sometimes, right? Instead of always hopping online, turning on the TV, listening to music, or whatever – the next time you're bored, open up God's Word. And, don't just take my encouragement to do it. St. Ambrose put it this way, "Why do you not use the time when you have nothing to do for reading or for prayer? Why do you not go and visit Christ our Lord and speak with Him and listen to Him? For when we pray we speak with God, and when we read, we listen to God." (28)
- Kiss it. For real. The next time you go to Mass, you will notice that the priest or deacon always kisses the Bible after reading the Gospel. Kissing is a powerful sign of love, intimacy, passion, and respect. Kissing the Bible is a great way to show God your love for Him and His Word. I dare you to try it either before you read it, after you read it, or both.
- Get a good one. OK, OK, so any Bible is a good one. (I can almost hear some people saying that to me right now.) What I am trying to say, though, is that you need to find one that meets your needs. There are many translations out there. I once heard a wise person say that the best translation of the Bible is the one you will read! Most of you probably do not need a version of the Bible in the original Greek or Hebrew languages. Some versions have a lot of words that we don't use too often in our daily conversations these days, either – like thee and thou and art and saith. As far as picking out a good Bible, I would recommend shopping around for a good Catholic youth Bible; you could just Google for "Catholic Youth Bible". Make sure it's Catholic, though, because Catholic Bibles contain 7 extra books that some Protestant Bibles don't; those books are really cool, too; and I wouldn't want you to miss out on them. And make sure it is a youth Bible because a good youth Bible will help you to apply the Scriptures to your daily life as a teenager. If you currently don't have a good Catholic youth Bible, and if you can't afford to buy one right now, start saving your money; it is an investment you won't regret. In the meantime, you could probably borrow one from your priest or youth minister or someone like that. If you have no regular source of income, or if you decide to spend your hard-earned income or allowance some other way, here is a crazy idea - ask your parents to buy you a Bible. You might need to wait for Christmas, your birthday, or some other special occasion, but I have never known a parent unwilling to buy a Bible for their son or daughter. If they are hesitant, tell them it will make you a better and more respectful teenager!

- Consider the Bible a love letter from God. Who doesn't enjoy a good love letter? You can even insert your name in key places to make it personal. Instead of John 3:16 simply being "God so loved the world that he gave His only begotten son..." why not read it as "God so loved <insert your name here>..." That is pretty powerful, and it makes it far more personal.

- Pick a time. Just like daily prayer time, it is good to have a consistent Bible reading time every day. Some people read the Bible as a part of their personal prayer time. Some people talk to God in the morning and read the Bible at night. Or, vice versa. Some people even bring their Bible to school and read it during free time - after completing an assignment, during study hall, or on the bus. It might sound kind of crazy, but it would be a powerful way to witness to your faith. Some people bring their Bible to work and read a little bit during their lunch hour. Regardless, it is a good idea to try to have some time set aside every day to read the Bible. Someone once said, "A Bible that is falling apart is usually owned by someone who isn't." (29) I like that quote so much, I actually wrote it in the front of my Bible. Will you?

- Get a study guide or devotional book. There are great study guides out there that help you to apply the Bible to every day situations. (30)

- Read it online. Even if you don't have Internet access at home, you can always get on the Internet at your local public library (31).

- Check out the topical index; most Bibles have one at the end, with Scriptures for you to look up that can apply to any mood or situation you might be in – happy, sad, grateful, angry, scared, tired, etc. If you check out a topical index, you will be blown away by all of the ways that the Bible speaks to our everyday lives.

- Mark it up. I promise it is not sacrilegious. Some of the holiest people I know have used highlighters (just make sure it doesn't 'bleed through' the pages) to mark their favorite passages and write comments in the margins of their Bibles.

- Memorize. I once had a friend who knew every line of the movie *Tommy Boy* by heart; she loved that movie and had seen it so many times that she could actually recite every line from memory. If people can do that with movies, why not with God's Word? Memorizing parts of Scripture is actually far more significant, life-changing, and eternally beneficial than knowing movie quotes. When you read the Bible and a passage seems to leap off of the page and really speaks to your heart, try to commit it to memory. Put it on a post-it note on your mirror; encourage a friend to memorize it with you. Test one another. If you memorize Bible passages, then those passages will come back to your mind later in life when you really need them. One of my favorites that I recall when I am feeling weak or overwhelmed is, "I can do all things through Christ who strengthens me." (32) One of my wife's favorites is, "In the world you will have trouble, but take courage, I have conquered the world." (33) I cannot tell you how much these verses have comforted and encouraged us through difficult times.

- Check out the Daily Mass Readings. There are several places online where you can find them, and many parishes print them in their weekly bulletin. What is awesome about reading and praying about the Daily Mass Readings is that (with some minor exceptions) Catholics throughout the entire world hear and read the very same readings each day. Therefore, it would be fair to say that these Scripture passages from Daily Mass are God's Word to the Catholic world, and that is pretty powerful. How cool is it that people in Africa, Australia, South America, and even Rome hear the same message from God every day? This is one thing I totally love about being Catholic, which literally means "Universal". I wonder if yet undiscovered life forms in other solar systems and galaxies have the same daily Mass readings...

Now that I have given you some tips for reading the Bible, I also want to share with you a couple of traps to avoid –

• Beware of reading from beginning to end. Shortly after I made a new commitment to Christ, I asked my parents for a Bible for Christmas. This totally surprised them, by the way; but they did buy me one. I was totally on fire to learn as much about God as I could by reading His Word, and so I decided to read the Bible from the beginning to the end. I started with Genesis and hoped to finish the Book of Revelation within a couple of months. Now this way of reading the Bible may work for some people, but it didn't work for me. Here's why. First of all, I was reading it wrong. The Bible is not a task to be accomplished, like completing a science project or running a marathon – it is a means of developing a relationship with a friend. There is no need to be in a hurry when reading the Bible. We should take our time and savor what God is saying to us, even if we only read one line or one word each day. It is supposed to be about listening, learning, meditating, and incorporating what we learn into our lives and relationships. I have heard it said (and I tend to agree) that it could be more beneficial to spend a month reflecting on one paragraph of the Bible than reading the whole thing in one year. You see, when I tried reading it from beginning to end, I got bogged down and pretty discouraged in the Book of Exodus. Sadly, I gave up. It is not a bad idea to read the entire Bible; it just needs to be done carefully. There are actually even some great guides out there to help people to read the entire Bible in a year. (34) If you check them out, you'll see that most of them mix it up with Old and New Testament passages in a way that helps to keep one's attention, and very few of these guides (if any) ask us to read the Bible from beginning to end.

• Don't only do "Bible Roulette". Bible Roulette is what I call the practice of just picking up a Bible and randomly flipping to a page and hoping for some inspiration. I know that this is a favorite way for some people to read the Bible, and I certainly am not totally against this way of reading God's Word. I know for sure that God can speak (and has spoken) to many people in this way. This kind of Bible reading even converted St. Augustine (his story is told in the chapter called "Shut Up!"), so I know it can be awesome sometimes. However, I believe that this should not be the only way to read the Bible. We will get more out of it if we put more into it by studying it, perhaps even a chapter or a book at a time. And, Bible Roulette can potentially misfire, which I will illustrate with my favorite Bible joke –

A man was playing Bible Roulette one day. He asked God to speak to his heart, and then he randomly flipped to a page where he randomly dropped his finger to a passage that read, "...he (Judas) departed and went off and hanged himself." (35) The man thought to himself, "God, I know that wasn't you. I am going to give you another chance!" So, again, he randomly flipped to a page where he randomly dropped his finger to a passage that read, "Jesus said...'Go and do likewise.'" (36)

- Don't think you know it all. There is a danger in thinking that any one of us can completely understand the entire Bible by ourselves. Although we can (and should!) read the Bible by ourselves for wisdom and inspiration, we also need guidance in understanding God's Word. There are a couple of reasons for this. For one, some passages can be confusing at first glance. For another, the Bible was written by people who, though under the inspiration of the Holy Spirit, lived in a certain time and place in history which influenced them. Also, there are certain types of literature in the Bible, and it is important to know the difference between a book that is poetry, parable, or historically factual information. We don't even need to know it all, and this is one of the gifts of being Catholic. We not only have the Bible, but right alongside God's Word we have nearly 2000 years of pastoral wisdom to help us apply the Bible to our daily lives. For these reasons, I encourage you to check out the footnotes in your Bible. And, if you want to take your understanding of the Bible to a deeper level, find reliable Catholic Scripture study guides; there are even online Catholic Bible study guides. You might even consider joining a Bible study group or starting a Bible study of your own. Checking out the wisdom God has given to us through others will help you to understand God's Word more fully. (37)

I think I will stop here. I encourage you to do the same. Take a break from my book and read God's book. I encourage you to begin with the Gospel of Mark. It is the shortest Gospel and has a lot to reveal to us about Jesus! Be sure to ask the Holy Spirit to speak to your heart as you read, and take your time. There is no hurry at all. I hope that you, like Emily, can discover how God sees you - and that you are never ugly to the One whose opinion matters most.

The "F" Word

The ten-year old girl went to bed that night just like she had every other night, not knowing that something was about to happen that would change her life forever. Sometime in the middle of the night, after being fast asleep, she suddenly woke up, totally confused and in extreme pain. He was on top of her, and she had no idea what was happening. She tried to scream for help, but no sounds came out of her mouth. He finished what he had begun and quietly slipped away, while she slowly cried herself back to sleep. When she woke up the next morning, she couldn't believe what had happened to her and wasn't sure if anyone else would believe it either. Who would believe that her brother's best friend had raped her? Unsure of what to do about it, she did nothing, except bury the memories of that night deep in her heart, where they remained - until puberty began, her hormones awoke, her body began to change, and the memories flooded back to her. Summoning all of her courage, she finally told a teacher, who convinced her to tell her parents, who brought her to a counselor. After just one counseling session, she told everyone that she was fine; and they believed her. But she wasn't fine. As a teenager, she responded to the trauma of her sexual abuse by avoiding relationships with guys. As she got older, especially in college, she became sexually active, sleeping with quite a few guys in an attempt to fill up the holes in her heart. Her untreated wounds eventually resulted in her developing an eating disorder. Later, as a young mother with beautiful children and an amazing husband, she became a very unhappy and completely lost soul. Her life began to spiral out of control. To the outside world she looked fine, but on the inside she was dying - in large part because of what had happened to her when she was ten years old.

What changed her life forever was her decision to get help. She started going back to church and receiving the sacraments. She entered counseling and joined a support group. And, with God's grace and a lot of prayer, she found the ability to do what some people might think impossible – she was able to forgive (yes, the "F" word!) the young man who raped her. She now prays for him, and even wishes him well in life, because she knows that only a very sick individual could have done to her what he did; she actually now has compassion for him. Recently she became a youth minister, and she is now devoting much of her time to helping troubled teens – because she knows what it is like to be lost and have a deeply wounded heart. She knows both sides of the issue: how forgiveness can bring real freedom, and how unforgiveness can keep someone enslaved. She once shared with me a quote that totally changed her life; "Resentment (unforgiveness) is like taking poison and waiting for the other person to die". (38) I don't believe that any of us really wants a heart full of poison, and that is why we all need the "F" word. That's right, we all need forgiveness. We all desperately need to be forgiven for the things we have done wrong, which I have dealt with in another part of this book. This chapter, however, is about forgiving others, even if the journey (like that of my friend) is a difficult one. Forgiveness is a tremendous gift from God that He wants us all to have. Before I describe in some detail what forgiveness is, and isn't, I want to share with you the story of another hero of mine in the area of forgiveness.

He was a sad young man, familiar with loss. His mother died when he was nine years old, and he lost his older brother three years later. His father died when he was twenty-one. As he grew up, though, he held on to his faith - and in so doing he let God take hold of him. He always loved God, who became his father; and he even developed a special relationship with Mary (the mother of Jesus) who became His mother: both of these relationships helped to fill the emptiness in his heart. Over time, as he grew in wisdom and maturity, he joined the priesthood and became a very strong leader in the church. He became a spiritual father to many, even though he had lost his earthly father as a very young child. A kind and compassionate man with great 'people skills', he loved to mingle. At every possible opportunity he wanted to share God's love with those he encountered. One day, while sharing the message of God's love with a large group of people, another man pulled out a gun and shot him. He was rushed to the hospital, and surgery was performed on his critical injury. It took him a long time to recover, but he eventually did; and he always believed that Mary had saved his life. Around two and a half years after the assassination attempt, he had the opportunity to meet his would-be assassin. What would he say to the man who tried to kill him? What would you say?

The man who was shot was Pope John Paul II, and the man who tried to kill him was Mehmet Ali Agca. Pictures were taken of this famous meeting, giving us images that the world will never forget. (39) The two men spoke privately for 20 minutes, and John Paul II later described the encounter, saying, "What we talked about will have to remain a secret between him and me. I spoke to him as a brother whom I have pardoned and who has my complete trust." (40) This powerful act of forgiveness prompted a Christian musician to write one of my all-time favorite song lyrics -

> I saw a man
> He was holding the hand
> That had fired a gun at his heart. (41)

It may seem like an impossible task to forgive someone who has committed the horrible act of sexual abuse, or someone who has tried to murder you. I suspect that some of you reading this right now have been hurt so deeply that you're not sure if you will ever be able to forgive whoever wounded (and perhaps is still wounding) your heart. If you feel that way, know that God loves you and understands your pain. He has suffered with you, and He is patient and kind. Forgiveness is a journey, and for some people it is a lifelong journey. I want to simply encourage you to begin the journey, since I know firsthand that there is an incredible amount of peace and joy when we reach the destination. If forgiveness is hard for you, perhaps you could start the process by simply asking God, "Please help me to be willing to begin to forgive." If you can even just pray that, I believe that your ability to forgive others will grow from there.

Even though forgiveness can be difficult, it is definitely possible. As the angel said to Mary once, "...nothing will be impossible for God." (42) And, that is the key. With God in our hearts, as we rely on His grace and power within us, forgiveness is not only possible - it is actually necessary for us to become the people that we have been created to be, free from past hurts and free to live an abundant life now and in the future.

My role models for forgiveness are not only the two awesome people that I just described to you, but also Jesus, who was actually the inspiration and role model for each of them. I have not been hurt as deeply as some of my friends have, and I certainly have not been hurt as deeply as Jesus was. But I do have my issues with people who have hurt me, and I am sure that you have yours. I know that forgiveness is often not easy, but I have learned that when forgiveness is hard for me, I recall the words that Jesus cried out from the Cross, "Father, forgive them, they know not what they do!" (43) Those words become my prayer. Uniting myself to Jesus really helps me as I strive to forgive others.

I want to be completely honest with you. Forgiveness does not mean that the painful things that have happened to us were OK, that they were no big deal, or that we have to accept that it was "God's will" for us to get hurt by other people or by the stuff of life. And I do not believe that we, as humans, can "forgive and forget" - I actually hate it when people toss around that phrase, and I consider it a lie straight from hell. When we forgive, it means that we are totally honest about our pain; we admit that it hurt deeply. It is nearly impossible to erase from our minds the powerful memories of when we have been hurt by others. Will Jesus ever forget the wounds He experienced on Calvary? Of course not, but He forgave his tormenters even as it was happening. Like Jesus, we can forgive; and in so doing we can let go of the anger, resentment, and bitterness. To me, it is very powerful that His wounds are now glorified and have become the source of healing for the world. Similarly, our wounds can become the source of healing for others when we allow God to touch and heal them. Who better to help the recovering alcoholic than someone who has been there? On countless retreats I have attended, someone's personal testimony of healing and forgiveness has given hope to people who are in a similar situation. How cool is that! We can even allow the Lord to transform and heal our painful memories, which you can learn more about in the chapter of this book called "The Worst Memory Ever."

In order for forgiveness to extend its roots deep into our hearts, we need to remember that forgiveness is a decision, one of the most important decisions we can make in our lives. To achieve forgiveness may require taking advantage of all of the spiritual resources at our disposal, including counseling, therapy, spiritual direction, and regular reception of the sacraments of Eucharist and Reconciliation. As we pursue forgiveness, though, we need to remember that we are not alone. God can help us, and God will help us, if we only ask for His help.

The "F" word can change each one of our lives, and it has the potential to change our world. Let's pray – "Jesus, help us to be people of forgiveness. Help us to be more like you."

Sacred Moments
(like winning the World Series)

I'm from St. Louis, which makes me one of the greatest fans in baseball. And, as you may know, the 2006 season was a very good season for us; we won the World Series! It was completely awesome.

Whether or not you are a St. Louis Cardinals fan, you probably have a favorite sports team. Right? Well, you can substitute an alternate team for this comparison (if you must), but I'm going to talk about the Cardinals because they're my team.

I'd like to ask you to go back, in your imagination, to the time that the Cardinals were in the World Series. Are you there yet? Good. Now, pretend that a friend of yours calls you up and offers you a ticket to one of the games. Would you take it? Well, heck yeah! And then your friend calls you right back to clarify, "By the way, I forgot to tell you that your ticket is for one of the dark-green seats; you know, the best and most expensive seats in the house, right behind home plate." It just couldn't get much better than that, could it? But maybe it could, because it ends up that on this particular night they win the Series, and you are even able to get your St. Louis Cardinals 2006 World Series Championship t-shirt signed by David Eckstein, the World Series MVP. If you have a good imagination, I'm pretty sure you feel the excitement of this once-in-a-lifetime opportunity. Right?

Now, I want to ask you (and myself) a very challenging question. Do we get that excited every weekend when we go to Mass? I mean, God created everything, including the Cardinals, so we must be that enthusiastic to go to Mass. Right? I think if we're honest, however, most of us would have to admit that we are not as excited about going to Mass every weekend as we are about rooting for our favorite sports team. Sadly, the opposite is often true; our churches are often quite empty and can even seem emotionally dead. Very few of us place the same priority on worshipping God as we do on going to a baseball game, and rarely do we hear anyone respond to the prayers or sing as enthusiastically for God as we would hear applause for a game-winning home run in our favorite stadium. Wouldn't it be awesome, though, if our churches were as full as our stadiums, with people showing the same enthusiasm for worshipping God as they do for a World Series victory? Maybe we just all need to be reminded that our best friend Jesus is there at church, and He definitely knows each one of us more personally and loves us more than any baseball player ever could. Do we even begin to comprehend what it is that we receive every time we go to church? It's something even better than getting a shirt signed by David Eckstein, and it happens every time: we get our hearts personally autographed by our Creator when we receive Jesus in the Eucharist. (44) Yes, the One who created everything out of nothing humbles Himself, coming to us in the form of a small piece of bread, to nourish our hearts.

You see, in Communion we receive Jesus. Not just a symbol of Jesus, but the real Jesus – body, blood, soul and divinity (45). As someone once said, "We hold in our hands He who holds the whole world in His hands." (46) Meditate on that quote for a while.

Some people have trouble understanding how the bread and wine could actually become Jesus. If you are one of those people, I want to share with you an analogy that really helped me to understand this a little bit better when I was struggling with the same issue of unbelief -

> *If you knew a piece of bread had been exposed to radiation for several minutes, would you eat it? I hope not! You see, exposure to radiation would change the bread so that by eating it you would actually be eating radiation, which would make you sick and perhaps even kill you. Any scientist would tell you that the change has taken place on an atomic level, which our senses cannot perceive. However, it still looks like bread; it still tastes like bread. Similarly, at the words of consecration ("this is my body" and "this is my blood") at Mass, God transforms what will still look like bread and wine and will still taste like bread and wine into the Body and Blood of Christ. This change takes place on a level that our senses cannot comprehend, but we are not trusting in a mere scientist for this knowledge; we are trusting in the promise of Jesus himself. And when we consume the Body and Blood of Christ - in complete contrast to eating what was exposed to radiation – we do not get sick or die, but we actually receive eternal life! (47)*

This analogy is completely awesome and really helps me to understand! If, on a natural level like this, bread can be changed without altering its appearance, why not on a supernatural level, by the God who is always trying to connect with us? Especially when the Scriptures are so clear that giving us His risen Body and Blood is something that Jesus wants to do –

> *I am the living bread that came down from heaven; whoever eats this bread will live forever; and the bread that I will give is my flesh for the life of the world." The Jews quarreled among themselves, saying, "How can this man give us (his) flesh to eat?" Jesus said to them, "Amen, amen, I say to you, unless you eat the flesh of the Son of Man and drink his blood, you do not have life within you. Whoever eats my flesh and drinks my blood has eternal life, and I will raise him on the last day. For my flesh is true food, and my blood is true drink. (48)*

and

> *While they were eating, Jesus took bread, said the blessing, broke it, and giving it to his disciples said, "Take and eat; this is my body." Then he took a cup, gave thanks, and gave it to them, saying, "Drink from it, all of you, for this is my blood of the covenant, which will be shed on behalf of many for the forgiveness of sins. (49)*

Yes, the Eucharist is really Jesus. He said so, and I trust Him 100%.

I once visited a church in another town; taped to all exit doors were signs that read "Even Judas Left Early." Ouch. Kind of harsh, I'd say. But the signs were probably put there by a leader at that church who was frustrated at how many people had been leaving Mass early, right after Communion. And I can understand that frustration, especially when I go back to the baseball analogy. If a World Series game was tied, and if the Cardinals had to go into extra innings, would you leave the game early? Neither would I! Yet many people leave Mass early (for a wide variety of reasons, including baseball games) even though something far more important than a baseball game is happening in church at Mass. (50)

I am far from perfect; and even as an adult, I need help and practical advice for getting the most out of Mass. I was once on a retreat (so long ago that I cannot remember where it was or who was speaking), but in the midst of listening to many words, I heard one thing that jumped out at me and spoke to my heart in a way that I will never forget; it was one of the greatest tips I have ever received for getting more out of Mass. The speaker challenged us to spend at least some of the time immediately after receiving Communion with eyes closed and hearts open, talking to Jesus who has just come into our hearts – instead of spending the whole time 'watching the parade'. You know what I'm talking about, right? It is so easy just to sit there after Communion and watch the parade of people returning to their pews. Believe me; I'm not trying to put you on a guilt trip for doing that, since I still watch some of the parade every Sunday. It's human and perfectly normal to want to notice who is there, and then try to wave, wink, or make faces at our friends. Some guys are checking out the pretty girls, and some girls are not only checking out the cute boys but they are also keeping an internal running commentary on the outfits that people are wearing (women in my life have told me this is true). Sure, this is normal, and it's what most of us do. But what should we be doing? I think that retreat speaker was correct; and so, ever since I heard that advice, I try to spend at least some of the time after Communion with my eyes closed and my heart open, talking to (or just being with) Jesus. Just for fun, let's take it back to baseball. If Albert Pujols came to my home for a visit, would I just stare out the window at traffic or at the people walking down my street while he was in my house? Of course not! I would want to hang out and chat with him. Well, in much the same way, someone cooler than Albert Pujols has entered into my heart during Holy Communion - the One who loves me more than I can imagine. And I am just beginning to understand how rude it might be when I spend the whole time 'watching the parade' instead of talking to my Best Friend.

I have a funny feeling that you might be reading this and thinking, "Yeah, Paul, I get it and all; but baseball games are much more exciting than Mass. You know what I am saying, right? Mass is BORING!" If that is what you are thinking, I appreciate your honesty. I have been where you are, and I have to be honest right back atcha - sometimes it is still a struggle for me to stay completely focused at Mass – not only because I sometimes wonder if I might be undiagnosed ADD, but because so much of what happens at Mass is repetitive. And repetition is boring, right? Not necessarily, my good friend! Two big insights have helped me to realize that the repetitious nature of the

Mass is in fact an awesome thing – first, because the Mass is universal, and second, because repetition is the language of love. To wrap up this chapter, I want to spend just a little time with each of these concepts.

First of all, the Mass is universal. One of the coolest things I ever discovered about the Mass is that it is not only Catholic but that it is catholic; as I noted before, the word *catholic* literally means *universal*. What this means is that (apart from a few minor exceptions) the Mass is celebrated in the same way, every day, in every corner of the world, even down to the same readings. I don't know about you, but that thought simply blows my mind. That means that whether someone goes to Mass this coming Sunday in St. Louis, Rome, Australia, Ethiopia, or Antarctica, the Mass is pretty much the same Mass in each place. Of course, it may be in a different language; but the essence of the Mass is the same – the same prayers, the same readings, the same blessings, the same Eucharist. I really like that; it helps me to realize that I am part of something much bigger than myself; so when I am worshipping God on the weekends, I am literally united in prayer with people on all parts of the planet. Whoa. Dude...

And, secondly, the Mass is God's language of love. A friend of mine reminded me a while ago that repetition is actually the language of love. (51) Imagine, if you will, the perfect boyfriend or girlfriend or spouse. OK, stop imagining...get back to reading; but keep that idea of a perfect romantic interest in the back of your mind. Do you really think that when you find someone who totally loves you for who you are that you will ever get bored with having that person express their love to you? Let me answer the question for you – NO! Love is absolutely not boring, even in its repetition and sameness. Trust me, as someone who is happily married, I never get tired of telling my wife how much I love her, and of hearing her say the same thing to me. And, of course, I never get tired of holding her hand, hugging, snuggling, kissing, and being intimate with her – even if I have done those same things hundreds and even thousands of times in our marriage – because those words and actions are the best ways that I can express my love for her! Now, in the Bible, Jesus actually referred to Himself as the Bridegroom and we, the Church, as His Bride. (52) In the Eucharist, Jesus gives Himself to us more completely and intimately than husbands and wives could ever give of themselves to one another - because God, who is perfect, unites Himself to us. And therefore the most loving thing we can do in response to His perfect gift to us is simply this - to give our lives completely to Him. The Mass is God's highest expression of love for us, since it contains all of the most perfect words and actions of intimacy that God could ever convey. And in response, our words and actions at Mass have been discerned by the Church to be the most perfect, loving, and thorough response we could ever give back to God. If you remember that every time you go to Mass, it will never be boring.

I Reckon' So

Sometimes I really enjoy a good Western movie, and one of my favorites is a Clint Eastwood classic called *The Outlaw Josie Wales*. So one night when my wife and daughter were occupied with more feminine activities, and when it was just the boys and me, we decided to have a guys' movie night and popped in the DVD. In case you haven't seen the movie, Josie Wales is a stoic, a man of few words. Throughout the movie, as a standard response to almost anything, he spits and says, "I reckon' so." Well, when the movie was over, my oldest son Jacob invented one of my favorite original, on-the-spot jokes. "What is the Outlaw Josie Wales' favorite sacrament?" he asked. The answer, "I reckon'-ciliation!"

Not only did I want to begin this chapter with that joke because I like it, but because the Outlaw Josie Wales really needed the sacrament of Reconciliation, as did most of the people in that movie. And so do I.

I think in a very real sense we are all outlaws, maybe not gunslingers like Josie Wales, but outlaws nonetheless. We have all broken the law of love. All of us have not only fallen short of loving one another well, but all of us have also fallen short of loving and obeying God as we should. The band Switchfoot puts it like this in their song, "Amateur Lovers" –

> *We don't know what we're doing*
> *We do it again*
> *We're just amateur lovers*
> *With amateur friends (53)*

To me this just means that none of us really have this "love" thing figured out. St. Paul put in this way in one of his letters –

> *...all have sinned and are deprived of the glory of God. (54)*

I know that I am probably stating the obvious. I think we are all pretty aware, most of the time, of our weaknesses, imperfections, and sins. But why do we, like Josey Wales, need the sacrament of Reconciliation? Many people in today's world don't think it is very important; it is a sacrament that is not received very often by most Catholics nowadays. And while there are many reasons that people don't go to Confession, I think the primary objection comes in the form of a question like this, "Why can't I just confess my sins directly to God and ask Him to forgive me? Why do I need to go to a priest?"

First of all, of course, we can and should confess our sins directly to God. Asking God directly for forgiveness happens during every Mass (Lord, have mercy!) and every time we say the Our Father (forgive us our trespasses); and of course we can ask for God's forgiveness any time we pray. However, the Catholic Church actually teaches that in addition to asking God directly for forgiveness, the sacrament of Reconciliation is also extremely important, so important that we are asked, as Catholics, to go at least once a year (55) – and more often is, of course, better! So I'd like to answer the question of why we should confess our sins to a priest in this sacrament by giving you an answer on three different levels – personal, psychological, and historical.

Personally, I just love this sacrament, even when I hate it, which I sometimes do. I'll be honest; sitting down and being completely honest with someone about the mistakes I've made and the sins I have committed does not rank super-high on my list of favorite things to do; and it probably doesn't for you, either. But my personal experience is that I always feel like a brand new person when I leave the sacrament. It's like when I was a little kid playing sports and had the chance for a "do over." I get a "do over" on life every time I receive this sacrament. I don't know about you, but my heart feels lighter, I am happier, and there is more joy in my heart right after Confession. Just hearing those words from the priest, "I absolve you from your sins in the name of the Father and of the Son and of the Holy Spirit," gives me confidence that I am, indeed, forgiven. There is something awesome about hearing these words spoken out loud by the priest, and that is something that I just don't get when I just confess my sins directly to God in my personal prayer time. I also want to share with you something I do which I really like - I go face-to-face, to the same priest, almost every time I go to Confession. I like to regularly receive the sacrament from this particular priest because I know he is an amazing priest, because I know He loves this sacrament, and because I trust him. He also happens to be my spiritual director (someone I meet with regularly to discuss my relationship with God), so that really works out well for me. I know other people who prefer going to Confession to a total stranger, because they prefer to be anonymous. Either way is cool with God. But, to me, the experience of this sacrament is beyond words. If it has been a while since you have felt those feelings of being completely forgiven and having a new lease on life, I encourage you to go. As a matter of fact, even as I write this chapter, I feel a tug at my heart to go to Confession soon. I am now going to share with you two other reasons this sacrament is essential for us Catholics, but please know that these other reasons are not separate from my personal reasons for going; they are intimately connected.

The psychological benefits of going to Reconciliation are beyond measure. I have heard it said that if Catholics would regularly receive the sacrament that billions of dollars could be saved every year on counseling bills! The reason is this – what we do in this sacrament is talk about our sins and problems to someone that we can trust, in a safe environment, where we can receive wisdom and encouragement to better our lives. That is precisely what we do in counseling, except in the sacrament we get something more – we encounter Jesus, who forgives our sins through the priest. There still may be times when we need counseling; and if you ever think you need to talk to a counselor, or if people who love you encourage you to get counseling, then please go! However, always combine counseling with the sacrament of Reconciliation – because both are tremendous ways to become better people when we are going through difficult times, which happens frequently in this crazy world of ours. This sacrament will help you to become a better and more mature person. It helps you to stay humble, since there is nothing more humbling than confessing your sins out loud. It also keeps us aware of our need for God and His mercy; and when we are recipients of mercy, we tend to be more merciful toward others. The key to experiencing these - and other psychological benefits - is to receive the sacrament regularly and prayerfully.

The historical reasons for receiving this sacrament are important to me, too. First of all, the sacrament of Reconciliation is referenced in the Bible as a gift that Jesus gave to his disciples when he said to them, "Whose sins you forgive are forgiven them..." (56). As Catholics we believe that this same authority has been passed down since the time of Jesus through his priests. Then there is this great promise from the book of James, "If we acknowledge our sins, he is faithful and just and will forgive our sins and cleanse us from every wrongdoing." (57) In addition to these reasons from the Bible, another reason that I feel so convinced of the importance of this sacrament is because it is what the early Church believed (58) and what the Church has consistently taught to be true, which is pretty cool when you consider that Jesus promised, "I am with you always, until the end of the age." (59)

As this chapter nears completion, I want to offer you some practical tips for receiving this sacrament.

1) If you feel a tug at your heart to go, go soon! Sometimes God gives us special encouragement to go (perhaps even through this book chapter), so it is important to respond to that 'prompting' when God gives it.

2) If it has been a long time and if you feel awkward or have forgotten how to go to Confession, just let the priest know that at the beginning. He will guide you through the process; that is what he is trained to do. He knows that the most important thing is not that you have all of the right words memorized, but that you want to get right with God!

3) Receive this sacrament regularly. I have heard some spiritual leaders suggest that we Catholics should receive this sacrament *at least* every six months, though more often is even better. It's kind of like how the dentist wants to see patients every six months, even if they might feel that nothing is seriously wrong. This trained professional checks us out to make sure that it's "all good" and wants us there for general cleaning and preventive maintenance. Regular Confession is exactly like that; it keeps our hearts clean and keeps wide open the lines of communication between us and God.

4) It is an excellent practice to make what the church calls an "examination of conscience" before receiving this sacrament. This simply means taking inventory of what you have done wrong so that your Confession is thorough. You can find a pretty good examination of conscience that is based on the Ten Commandments online at www.reapteam.org/examination-of-conscience

Please keep in mind that if receiving the sacrament of reconciliation is sometimes hard for you, you are not alone. It is still sometimes difficult for me, too. But it is worth it! You see, I have learned that the older I get, what is right is not always easy, and what is easy is not always right. Yet when I have the courage to humbly seek God's mercy, He forgives, and I am healed. I encourage you to ask God for the grace to be open to this powerful sacrament. Will you be glad you asked? I reckon' so.

Show Me...Your Future

I live in Missouri, and our state nickname is "The Show Me State". That means that we tend to be skeptical; we know that words are cheap and that actions speak louder than words. In other words, you can tell me that you love me, but I will know that for sure when you show me some love. I also know you can promise to be there for me, but I will know for sure that you will when you actually show up for me in my time of need. The bottom line for a person from Missouri, then, is that you have to show me; that is when I will know 'fo sho' that something is real.

If you really want to live for Christ, I want to share with you a great way to show that your commitment to live for Him is real. It is through your choice of friends. Your choice of friends will, quite simply, show everyone what your priorities are; and it can even determine the direction of your life. A wise friend of mine is fond of saying –

Show me your friends, and I'll show you your future. (60)

I suspect that some of you just read that and feel awesome; you know that your future is bright because your friends are incredible, mask-free people who are role models of faith and love. And I suspect that some of you just read that line and are thinking, "Oh, snap! My future could be in trouble!"

I want to be very clear; I am not saying that we should be friends only with people who are living saints. Jesus certainly hung out with all kinds of people and was a friend of sinners, so in following Him we should befriend all kinds of people - including those who might lack faith and those who are making bad choices. However, Jesus did have his group of twelve disciples - those he was closest to - and he shared his life more deeply and intensely with them than anyone else on Earth. They were His support system, and that is what I am talking about - having a core group of people close to us that we can depend upon to be supportive of our faith and who share our values. To live the Christian life in today's world we need all the help we can get, and the encouragement of our peers is essential. St. John Bosco put it like this –

Fly from bad companions as from the bite of a poisonous snake.
If you keep good companions, I can assure you that you will one
day rejoice with the blessed in Heaven; whereas if you keep with
those who are bad, you will become bad yourself, and you will be
in danger of losing your soul. (61)

One of the bigger blessings of my life is that for over a dozen years I had the privilege of being an adult leader for a Catholic youth prayer group called God's Gang. Being a leader of this group changed my life, as well as the lives of most of the teenagers who faithfully attended. We met every Wednesday night for a couple of hours, and our format was simple. We began with music, praising and worshipping God. Then we had a commercial, which was a mini-teaching on some aspect of our faith. This was followed by a talk given by either a teen or adult; usually some discussion followed the talk. The meeting ended with some spontaneous prayers for our needs and the needs of others. Following the official meeting, we always had what we called 'fellowship time' – a Christianized way of saying we would hang out, drink soda, eat snacks, and chat.

A lot of teens came in and out of our group, but most of the teens who attended this group *on a regular basis* are still strong in their faith, and many have taken on leadership positions in our church and in the world. They have become music ministers, teachers, and youth ministers. Some have explored the priesthood and religious life. Others lead prayer groups, and many are faithful parents preparing the next generation of children to live for Christ. What made those who attended this youth group as teens such outstanding leaders today as adults is simply the fact that they made youth group a priority in their lives.

Of all of the teenagers I have ever met, the overwhelming majority of those who are strongest in their faith and who have managed to stay faithful to Christ are the ones who made youth group a priority. The kind of spiritual support a youth group offers is extremely important for three main reasons.

First of all, we live in a world where there are many forces opposed to faith; and these obstacles are encountered in an overwhelming way in middle school, high school, and college. If you have not yet encountered these things, you will soon. These temptations include, but are not limited to, pressure to do drugs, drink, cuss, fight, talk about other people, and be sexually impure. While it is always a battle to remain strong in faith and resist temptation, it is an undeniable fact that it is easier to live for Christ when we have the support of others. Though negative peer pressure is strong, positive peer pressure is far more powerful. Gathering in Christ with fellow believers can not only help us to resist temptation, but a good group of supportive friends can even help us to avoid places and situations where temptation might be strongest. And the reason for all of this power in communities of faith is because of what Jesus said so clearly,

>...*where two or three are gathered together in my name, there am I in the midst of them. (62)*

How about that? When we hang out with other believers, we automatically place ourselves in the presence of Jesus; and that is extremely powerful and completely cool. Think about it.

Second, youth groups set us up with activities that give us opportunities to learn more about faith and actually experience God's love, through a wide variety of things like prayer nights, teen Masses, retreats, talks, conferences, and service opportunities.

And third, youth groups are places where we can connect with trusted adults who really love us. Sometimes we have problems and questions that our friends cannot help us with, and the adult leaders of youth groups can be extremely helpful and insightful. I know lots of teens who have received invaluable help during hard times because they sought out the advice of youth group leaders.

For all of these reasons, if you are not part of a youth group right now, I want to encourage you with all of my heart to join one! And, if you are already a part of a youth group, I encourage you to keep on attending and strive to become one of its most faithful members. Because if you make youth group a priority, God will bless you in ways that you cannot even begin to imagine.

I realize that some of you reading this right now are thinking, "But, Paul, my church doesn't have a youth group!" If that's you, I want to encourage you to consider the following things:

1) Talk to your pastor
2) Start a youth group
3) Broaden your search

Talk to your pastor

If you don't have a youth group in your parish, I want to encourage you to talk to your pastor. I urge you to call him and ask for an appointment to meet with him face to face. Then, when you meet with him, begin by telling him about your faith; share your story with him. Let him know how you have come to know Jesus in a deeper and more personal way, and let him know that you want to grow even closer to God. Trust me; he might really need the inspiration and encouragement that will come from hearing about your faith! While you are at it, ask for his wisdom on how to strengthen your faith – he will probably give you some excellent advice on how to keep the Holy Spirit stirred up. Then, tell him that you are interested in being a part of a youth group and tell him why this is your desire. He may be aware of a youth group in your church or a nearby parish that you don't even know about. Or there may even be other teens and adults in your parish who want to start a youth group that he can tell you about.

Me, start a youth group?

My second suggestion is to start a youth group yourself, and it is not as crazy as it might seem. I remember once meeting a girl named Jess. Her parish had nothing to offer young people, so she started a teen prayer group – without the help of any adults. All she did was simply meet with several of her friends once a week, and this is what they did – they talked about their problems, checked to see what the Bible says about their problems, and then prayed for each other about their problems. That's a youth group! Your youth group does not need to be like Jess', either. Just spend some time thinking and praying about what you want in a youth group and then start talking to some of your like-minded friends about your ideas. Your group could focus on studying the Bible, on praying the rosary, on praise and worship, on going to Adoration, on spiritual accountability (see the chapter of this book called "An Indian Named Tonto"), or something else. Be creative; the possibilities are endless. You can get something started, if you really want to. And there are probably trusted adults that you know who could help you; ask your pastor if he knows of anyone. It just depends upon how badly you want to be part of a youth group.

How do I broaden my search?

Another thing you can always do is to broaden your search. When I was a leader for the youth group God's Gang, there were not a lot of youth groups in St. Louis with a spiritual focus. So, some students drove (or had their parents drive them) 45 minutes - one way - every Wednesday night to join us. They knew that youth group was important, and they were willing to travel to get the spiritual support they needed. If you live in or near a big city, there are youth groups out there, if you search for them. To find a youth group in your area, talk to your pastor, call your diocese's youth office, search the web, or just start asking around. Again, you may need to travel to get to a youth group; and if you don't have a car that can be difficult; but if you explain to some loving adults in your life why you want to go to a youth group, they'll probably help to get you there.

Still Nothing?

In some situations, there will be people who have tried everything that I have suggested so far in this chapter, yet they still cannot find a youth group or cannot get to one. If that is you, I just want to encourage you – hang in there and keep praying! Although it is difficult to follow Christ as a teen without being a part of a youth group, it is not impossible. Jesus Himself said,

...for God all things are possible (63)

He will sustain you if you remain faithful to praying, reading the Bible, and regularly receiving the sacraments of Eucharist and Reconciliation. And, while He is sustaining you, ask Him to continue to send you what you need. If you have a computer and an Internet connection (and even if you don't, your local library does!) you could even check out some online communities for Catholic teens. (64)

Choosing a Youth Group

If there is a youth group in your parish, I want to encourage you to join it – even if it is not yet everything you think you need. I have known of some teens who, even though their parish had a youth group, chose to go to another youth group at another parish. There are often very good reasons for this choice - they get more out of it, the other youth group is bigger, they like the adult leaders more, they have more friends there, it seems to be less cliquey, a member of the opposite sex they like goes there, there is better music, or the talks are more inspiring – in short, the other parish youth group is more attractive. Although I totally understand the desire to go to a group that meets your needs, I want to encourage you to consider this: a parish group quite simply cannot grow into what God wants it to be when good people won't stick around. And, as much as I love the mega youth groups out there, I know that their existence can be a drain upon smaller and start-up groups.

If you have this struggle, I want to propose a solution that I believe is a win-win situation to the big youth group/small youth group issue; and the solution is inspired by the example of my friend Jon. While Jon was in high school, he attended two youth groups. One was a large, vibrant youth group at another parish, where he was spiritually 'fed' and was an active member. The other group was a smaller, less vibrant youth group at his parish; but it was a group that needed his presence and his leadership. By attending both groups, Jon remained faithful to his parish, continued to grow in faith, and enjoyed the opportunities that God gave him to both give and receive. He reminds me of what someone once shared about the difference between the Red Sea and the Dead Sea. The Red Sea is teeming with life because there is water that flows both in and out. The Dead Sea is dead because water only flows in. In other words, if we are only giving or if we are only receiving when it comes to our spiritual life, we will not be nearly as alive as we could be.

Final Thought

I will end this chapter with the quote that I shared with you near the beginning –

Show me your friends, and I'll show you your future. (65)

I pray that you will always have really good friends and an excellent future, no matter where God leads you.

The Worst Memory Ever

Someone was giving a talk at a youth conference about how much God loves us, but the teenage girl just couldn't believe it. She walked out of the auditorium in tears. A friend of mine and I had the chance to talk to her, and between sobs she told us about her worst memory ever – a memory that was haunting her and blocking her ability to be open to God's love.

Her friend had recently committed suicide, and she was convinced that it was her fault. Her friend had called her one night while she was at church and said, "I am going to kill myself tonight. Do you want to come over and join me?" Since she thought that he was kidding, she responded with a sarcastic and joking tone, "Shut up and leave me alone. I hate you!" and hung up on him. Later that night, she was the first one to discover his lifeless body. He had actually done it; he had taken his own life by shooting himself in the head. She quickly realized that her words were perhaps the last words he had heard on Earth and that his phone call had actually been a cry for help. She believed she could have saved his life, but she didn't. Since that night, she had constantly second-guessed herself as to what she should have said and done. And she was tormented by the memory not only of what she had said to him from church but also by the discovery of his lifeless body. She was convinced deep in her heart that his death was her fault – that her words and inappropriate response had resulted in his committing suicide. She felt unworthy of God's love, especially when she was at church events, since she had been at a church event when her friend took his life.

As we talked, I assured her that it was not her fault – that if people really want to take their own life, no one can make them, and no one can stop them. (66) Those words were not enough, though. She had heard them countless times from friends and counselors, yet she still believed that it was her fault that her good friend was now dead.

I want to pause right now, in the middle of this true story, and let you know that I am one of those people who happen to believe that Jesus is not just some historical figure who used to touch and heal people 'back in the day' when He walked the Earth in the flesh. I believe that He still loves to show up and touch and heal His people, people like you and me, and people like this brokenhearted teenage girl. There are countless ways that Jesus can show up in our lives, but the one I want to share with you right now is absolutely amazing. It can change your life forever, as it did for this young woman. It is through a kind of prayer called "the healing of memories".

My friend and I began to pray with this young woman, and it became very clear that Jesus wanted to heal her memories of that night when her friend had committed suicide. Here is how He did it. As we prayed, we took her back into the experience and all of the memories of that night; she relived it all. She went back into the room and saw her friend's lifeless and bloodied body, and she cried and felt all of her original feelings. Then we asked Jesus to come into the scene. We imagined Him holding her friend's dead body in His arms, telling her, "It's OK now; it wasn't your fault. Your friend is with Me now." While still being held by Jesus, her friend's eyes opened, and he looked at her. Out loud, she asked for his forgiveness, and he gave it to her. He stood up, walked over to her, and gave her a hug. Jesus joined, and it became a group hug as he wrapped both of them in His arms. Jesus then took her friend by the hand, and they walked off together. By inviting Jesus into her worst memory ever, this brokenhearted teenager girl finally experienced a peace that she had not felt in a long time.

We all have bad memories because we live in a broken world where we all get hurt by other people or just by the 'stuff of life'. Do you have any bad memories from your past of something absolutely awful or extremely painful that happened to you or to someone you love? I know that I have memories like that, like the time I was in 6th grade and cried in class because I didn't like my teacher, or the time that I found out that a friend from college died in a motorcycle accident.

Did you know that Jesus wants to bring healing to those bad memories that you and I have? It's true. He has done it for me, and He can do it for you. Let me tell you how. As I have prayed about that time in 6th grade, I imagined Jesus being with me, with his arms around me, telling me that He loves me and that I will be OK. When I prayed about my friend who died in the motorcycle accident, I had an image in my mind of Jesus smiling, welcoming her into Heaven. These are simple and yet very powerful examples of how Jesus can heal our memories.

There are probably skeptics who would say that what happens with the healing of traumatic memories is just wishful thinking or playing make-believe. I disagree with all of my heart. Two Bible passages that provide a sound basis for the healing of memories are "Jesus is the same yesterday, today, and forever" (67) and Jesus' own words in the Book of Revelation, "Behold, I make all things new." (68) As people of faith, we believe that Jesus is everywhere, all of the time. And since we know that He is always with us, we can also trust that he has always been with us, every moment of our lives - especially in our most difficult times. The healing of memories is simply looking at the difficult times of our lives with the eyes of faith. If you ever have read the poem *Footprints* (69), then you know what I am talking about – in our toughest times of struggle and pain, God carries us.

What happens in the healing of memories is, in fact, **more real** than what happened the first time, because it is allowing God's perspective and truth to be infused into our lives. In Christ, there is always a bigger picture, and the healing of memories helps us to see that picture more clearly. It's also kind of like what happens in *The Lion, the Witch, and the Wardrobe,* where Aslan refers to a "Deeper Magic from before the dawn of time - a mercy that surpasses human understanding." (70) This deeper magic is God's truth about what happened, and God's love healing what has happened to us. We can trust His love and truth and mercy all of the time – even in the healing of memories.

I know someone who lost her husband way too soon in life. When he died, it left her devastated and her children fatherless. She shared with me once that she would often awaken at night, remembering the moment when the doctor said to her, "I have some bad news." The pain of a memory like this is beyond my ability to fathom, for I have never experienced a loss like hers. However, as she shared this with me, I felt compelled to share this idea of God's healing of memories with her. I encouraged her to do something very specific any time she recalls this memory, either in her sleep or while awake - to imagine

Jesus standing behind the doctor and adding, after the doctor has spoken, this powerful truth, "Yes, but I have some very good news for you. I am taking your husband to spend eternity with me, to a place where there is no more death, no more pain, and only love." This way of dealing with that memory has brought some healing to this woman's broken heart.

As I bring this chapter to a close, I have three more things to share with you about the healing of memories, and they are all very important.

First of all, the healing of memories does not take away all of our pain, but it does soften and transform the pain. The woman who lost her husband and the teenage girl who lost her friend to suicide are still in a lot of pain. They both still cry often and grieve deeply – as they should. But they have both realized that their pain is not the end of the story: their pain is not the final answer. It never is! The final answer to everything is what God has to say about it, and that is something that we can discover through the healing of memories. Second, keep in mind that for the really big hurts in life the healing of memories is just the beginning. As you think about your own memories that may need to be healed, ask God what more you should do. Often, we really need to share those most painful times in life with a trusted parent, youth minister, or counselor – someone who can listen well to what we have been through, pray with us, and give us good advice for ongoing healing.

Finally, as this chapter comes to an end, I want to ask you a very personal question. What are your worst and most painful memories? Would you be willing to go back to those memories and relive them, in order to let Jesus in? As you do, what do you see Jesus doing? What does He have to say to you? After Jesus touches your memory, be sure to share the good news of what He has done for you with someone you really trust; and if you want to share the good news with me, you can let me know by sending me an email through this book's website.

Know that I am praying for you, praying that you might allow Jesus to heal your memories. If this healing of memories stuff intrigues you, check out the appendix called "Prayer for Healing of Memories." It is a great prayer that you can either pray by yourself, have someone pray with you, listen to, or download to your mp3 player.

Jon & Amber's Keg Party
(an incomplete chapter)

Jon, a junior in high school, was a starter for his high school soccer team, and his beautiful girlfriend Amber (a dancer) was a sophomore. The previous year Jon had attended the big beer bash with his whole soccer team after the annual grudge match against his school's archrivals. He had a good time, overall, at that party – he hung out with some good friends, listened to some good tunes, and had plenty to drink. He enjoyed talking about it afterwards – back at school in the hallways on Monday with his fellow partiers. However, thinking back on that experience, he still considered it kind of a lame party. He knew he could throw a better and crazier and wilder party than the one he had attended.

So the next school year Jon and Amber decided to throw a keg party that would put last year's party to shame. This would not just be another 'show up and drink' party for high school students. They planned it out meticulously. Fliers were made and passed out at school, they planned for and bought some good munchies, and they easily found someone over 21 that they trusted to reserve and pick up the keg for them. They even had party t-shirts made that they planned to sell to help cover the expense of throwing such a huge bash.

The night came for the party, and it was a huge success. Large numbers of people attended – some were people they knew, and some were total strangers. Gratefully, no one trashed the house. The police never showed up and busted the party, and no one got pulled over on the way home and got arrested. All of the t-shirts were sold, and that party was the talk of their high school the following Monday morning.

Regardless of what you think of Jon and Amber for throwing a keg party for their fellow high school students, you have to admit that they were driven – they wanted to do something with excellence, and they succeeded! Even though it was a couple of years ago, people are still talking about Jon and Amber's keg party.

Did I mention to you that at the time of this party, Jon and Amber were active in a ministry that gives retreats to other teens and that they were also active members of youth groups? In light of that, do you think that they are hypocrites for throwing such a party? Do you think that perhaps their youth ministers and parents were ashamed of their behavior? This may sound scandalous, but we are all very proud of Jon and Amber; and we consider them an inspiration to us and to their peers. You see, they pursued excellence, which inspires people. And, by the way, the t-shirts that they made said, "Intoxicated with Love." I also failed to mention earlier that the keg that was bought for their party was freely flowing with root beer, which the party guests drained to the last drop. That's right; their party was a *root beer kegger*.

What I love about Jon and Amber's story is that they saw a problem and decided to do something about it. At the high school they attended, they were simply sick and tired of always hearing so many people brag on Monday mornings about how they got so wasted on the weekends. Since Jon and Amber don't drink alcohol, they knew that you can have tons of fun without drinking and that if you don't drink you will have even more fun. Their problem was convincing their classmates, and the root beer kegger was the solution. Jon and Amber, by throwing this party, were excellent witnesses and servants of Jesus. Consider these quotes -

> *Every day I preach the Gospel, and sometimes I use words.*
> *--St. Francis of Assisi (71)*

> *What we practice, not (save at rare intervals) what we preach, is usually our greatest contribution to the conversion of others.*
> *--C.S. Lewis (72)*

> *Those who are silent about injustices are accomplices of them.*
> *--Father Oreste Benzi (73)*

> *Let us thank God that he makes us live among the present problems; it is no longer permitted to anyone to be mediocre.*
> *--Pope Pius XI (74)*

> *You know well enough that Our Lord does not look so much at the greatness of our actions, nor even at their difficulty, but at the love with which we do them.*
> *--St. Therese (75)*

I don't know about you, but I want to be like Jon and Amber – creative and extreme in how I witness to Jesus in this crazy world that we live in. Please know that they did not read the Bible to their party guests, they did not stop the party for a prayer meeting, and they did not pass out holy cards to people when they left the party. What they did was offer a healthy and fun alternative – which actually led some people to ask them later about their motives in throwing a party like this. When asked about those things, I know that they were not ashamed to tell people about Jesus and their faith and the value of being sober.

Sadly, there are some people who are very pessimistic about the world that we live in today. Even sadder, there are some people who are deeply discouraged about teenagers. Some people think that teens are mostly selfish, confused, lost, and hopeless individuals. I want to be very clear with you – I am not one of those people! And God certainly does not feel that way about you either! Though I am well aware of the problems and temptations that most teens encounter, I remain hopeful and confident in God's grace. I know that young people just like you can do amazing things for God and for this world. You are totally capable of loving God and other people passionately, listening intently for God's guidance, and responding to God's call with an energy and enthusiasm that most grown-ups lack.

Not only have I seen teenagers respond to God's grace countless times, like Jon and Amber did, but it happened to me when I was a teenager. Late in my teen years, after I had made a commitment to Christ, God began speaking to my heart about pursuing youth ministry. I began thinking more about it, praying about it, and checking it out until I gradually discovered that it was something that I not only really enjoyed doing, but also something that I was pretty good at. All of my past personal and educational experiences, good and bad, seemed to have prepared me for this career. Over time, with a lot of prayer and discussion with many wise people, it became very clear that youth ministry was in fact God's call for my life. God called me as a teenager, and I responded. I have been a youth minister now for over 20 years, and I have never regretted it for a moment. By listening to God, not only have I experienced a lot of peace and joy in my life, but I've also been able to share God's peace and joy with many others. I have had the chance to speak of God's love to thousands and thousands of teens, and many of them have responded – all because I listened to God and have allowed Him to work through me to reach others with His goodness, love, and blessings. I am just a small piece of the puzzle as to how God wants to reach this world with love, but I am an important piece – and so are you!

I want to encourage you to keep listening, and to prayerfully respond to what God calls you to do. God needs you to touch a very hurting and broken world with His love. How can you serve God in your family, your school, and your community? I'll tell you how - through community service!

Please don't start zoning out now that I am talking about community service. I want to be honest; I purposely avoided putting those two words "community service" in the title of this chapter precisely because I understand the temptation to zone out when you hear them. I even wonder if writing those words just now was such a great idea.

If you have 'attitude' about community service, join the club. I remember cringing when I was in 8th grade, preparing for Confirmation, when I was told I needed to do community service. You would have thought, based upon my reaction, that I had been asked to go down a slide covered with razor blades into a swimming pool filled with acid! That's how painful community service sounded to me.

I believe that a big problem with community service today is that so many people misunderstand it, because they are often required to do it – for Confirmation service hours, as a high school graduation requirement, or because they know it will look great on their job resume or college application. Now, these things are not bad – and I know for sure that the people who encourage (and even require us) to do community service have great intentions: they know that doing service to others makes us better people. However, if you are like me, attitude is everything. And when I am required to do something, when I have to do it, I can get the attitude that it is a burden and a hassle. Many of us have the attitude toward service that we have toward homework – we'll do it if we absolutely have to, but we would rather not; we have better things to do with our free time. If that is your attitude (and it used to be mine), then I want to encourage you to ask God to give you a serious "attitude adjustment". God can do that; and when God does, you will become animated by the Holy Spirit and begin to see community service as something you GET to do. Here is a big secret – find something that you are passionate about. You may need to do some experimenting; but if you do, you will eventually find something that is your gift and that brings joy to your heart while serving the community. It may be service to little kids, or the elderly, or the poor, or youth ministry, or something else. But when you discover the place where your passion meets the needs of others, you will be in a great place – for God, for His people, and for your own personal growth and development.

I know all kinds of young people who give up their free time (when they could be relaxing, reading, playing video games, or sleeping) - and greatly inconvenience themselves to do amazing acts of loving service. It's a kind of long list, so you can check it out in the appendix called "Nothing Like Going Down a Slide"... if you are interested.

I have personally known teens that have done all of these, and many other wonderful things for God, because they want to make a difference in this world. One thing I really admire about them is that they have overcome both laziness and fear, which are the biggest obstacles to discovering God's vision for your life and doing something significant with it. Even now, at the thought of doing something significant for God, some of you might be wondering, "What will others think of me? What will I have to give up? What will people say? Will my peers make fun of me?" I know I have asked those questions in my heart at various times in my life, and so have Jon, and Amber, and all the teens who have done the cool stuff you can find in the appendix – but they still stepped out in faith! What makes all the difference, though, is wondering more about things like, "What will God think of me? What will be the impact on other people? What will I gain? How can I make a difference in my world? How will I feel about myself if I don't do what I am being called to do?"

My favorite story of a young person who overcame fear is Mary of Nazareth. Can you imagine being an unmarried teenager and being asked by an angel if you would be willing to be the mother of God's only Son? Imagine the questions she asked herself, "What will people say about me? What will people think of me? What kinds of rumors will get started? Can I really do this? How is this possible?" The good news for the world, though, is that Mary did not listen to those discouraging voices. She listened to God, and she said yes. And, in saying yes, she brought Jesus into the world. Ladies and gentlemen, boys and girls - that is precisely what will happen when we, in our own unique way, in our own very unique circumstances, are willing to move past the discouraging voices, listen to God, and say yes. Each one of us can bring Jesus into our world. And that is something our world desperately needs.

One final thought. You may have noticed that the subtitle of this chapter is "an incomplete chapter". It is incomplete, because so is my life and your life. Your life has a special purpose, and there are some things that you – and only you - have been created to do. Not until you do those things will your life be complete. So, I have left the next page blank on purpose. You need to finish this chapter. I want to challenge you to spend some time listening to God, and perhaps even brainstorming with some of your friends and family members. Write down on this blank page some ideas of things that God might be calling you to do for Him and for His people - to bring Jesus to the world, just like Mary did. Then comes the most important thing – just get out there and do something!

And as you continue this chapter, know that it will not be complete until you meet Him. Face to face.

An Indian Named Tonto

When I was a child, I loved the TV show called "The Lone Ranger," a show about a cowboy in the Old West who always caught the bad guys. The Lone Ranger was super-cool; he always wore a black mask to disguise his real identity, and he rode a beautiful white horse named Silver. In my childhood imagination, I used to sometimes pretend that I was the Lone Ranger – a hero who would save the world (or at least my portion of it) from those who would seek to do wrong. One really interesting thing about the Lone Ranger is that there was this awesome Indian named Tonto who was his sidekick: he was always there to be his companion and to help him out in times of trouble.

When I think about trying to live the Christian life in today's world, the Lone Ranger speaks to me. No, not out loud; that would be weird! I guess I should rather say that the Lone Ranger inspires me. Because even though his name was The Lone Ranger, he still needed Tonto...

Get it? Well, allow me to explain. I think that, in one way, each of us might consider ourselves, and in fact might be, Lone Rangers. Although God has given us the gift of free will, it is ultimately up to us how we use that gift. We are free to do whatever we want with our time, talent, and treasure - and we are responsible for our own lives and the choices we make. Even so, I believe that in order to be truly successful and happy in this life, we need help, just like the Lone Ranger needed Tonto. Without Tonto, there were some messes that the Lone Ranger would not have been able to get out of. And there were lots of other problems that the Lone Ranger was able to avoid - because Tonto had his back.

Over the course of the past several years, this notion of the Lone Ranger needing Tonto has completely revitalized and deepened my relationship with God. The Lone Ranger was smarter than I am; he knew all along that he needed Tonto. But it took me far too long to figure out that, like the Lone Ranger, I needed a Tonto, too; actually, I need lots of Tonto's in my life. This principle of depending upon others to help me deepen my relationship with God is what I am going to call "spiritual accountability", but I will warn you right now that it is not for wimps, weaklings, or the faint of heart. And while it is very challenging, spiritual accountability has become one of the most valuable tools in my spiritual toolbox. In fact, it is a tool that I have found to be absolutely essential if I want to grow continually deeper in my relationship with Jesus, as well as in my relationships with other key people in my life.

Spiritual accountability is a very unique way of relating to others that I believe God wants each of us to experience; it can be with one person, several people, or a group. In this chapter I am going to use the term 'accountability partner' for the sake of simplicity, but keep in mind, as I said, that we can relate this way with several people or within a group setting. An accountability partner is someone to whom I give permission to encourage, challenge, and question me about every aspect of my personal, spiritual, and moral integrity. Such a relationship is difficult because it requires a decision to be totally transparent and completely vulnerable with another human being, something that most of us Lone Rangers would prefer not to do. However, the reason for having an accountability partner is so that we can constantly be growing in spiritual maturity, which I hope is a goal that we all have.

Choosing an accountability partner should be done carefully and prayerfully; but the bottom line is this – it simply must be someone who cares about you deeply and that you can trust to keep a secret, since much of what is shared with an accountability partner is deeply personal and private. This person should also ideally be the kind of person whom you plan on being close to throughout the years, rather than just a "friend for a season." Accountability partners should be mask-free people willing to ask the tough questions, but always out of a deep love and a desire to help you attain your ultimate goal of Heaven.

An accountability partner can be a peer or can be a trusted adult like a priest, religious sister, or youth minister. My strong personal opinion is that an accountability partner should be someone of the same sex - never a member of the opposite sex – since so much of what is shared within this relationship is about sensitive personal topics, including sexuality issues. Since accountability partners help us to grow into Christian womanhood or manhood, this kind of sharing is best done with the same sex, since we men can only learn how to be a real man from other men, and vice versa for the women. So, obviously, an accountability partner should not be a boyfriend or a girlfriend or husband or wife. And this is a great thing, because when a relationship with an accountability partner is completely open and honest, it will actually enhance a person's dating or marriage relationship – for anyone who is accountable to another human being will gradually become more spiritually healthy, more emotionally healthy, more connected to God, and therefore a more loving person.

A relationship with an accountability partner is one that is usually different from a relationship with a spiritual director (which is also important for spiritual growth), since a spiritual director is usually older and more mature in faith, while an accountability partner can be a peer. And, while most people decide for themselves how often they meet with a spiritual director, an accountability partner hopefully will be available 24/7. Additionally, in spiritual direction there is usually a specific focus on one's relationship with God, while accountability partners can ask you about anything. Finally, spiritual direction is often a more 'professional' relationship, like a spiritual physician you see for periodic check-ups. An accountability partner can be more of a like-minded friend who is given permission to check up on you any time at all.

Areas of accountability can include, but are certainly not limited to, our prayer life, our thought life, the quality and depth of our relationships, our moral integrity, and our sexual purity.

Brutal Honesty Required

An accountability partner is someone who helps you through the process of overcoming your sinful nature, just like a 'sponsor' helps someone going through a 12-step program to overcome their addiction. The first step in any good recovery program is to admit that we have a problem – and so an accountability partner is someone with whom I am willing to share my problems. For me, sharing my personal struggles with at least one other person (in addition to the priest I meet with for the Sacrament of Reconciliation) is very important because it keeps me humble. My father-in-law is fond of encouraging God's people to be brutally honest. I have heard him say things like,

> "It is tempting to be vague, saying things like 'I have had impure thoughts.' It is tougher, but much more freeing, to be specific. 'I lusted.' 'I masturbated.' 'I viewed pornography.' It is important that we call sin what it is."

So, are you willing to take inventory? Are you willing to be brutally honest as to what most keeps you from a deeper relationship with God? Is it an inconsistent prayer life, lack of scripture reading, laziness, or dysfunctional relationships? Is it something else? Ask God to show you, and He will. And while you are talking to God, ask Him this, "God, do you want me to have an accountability partner? If so, who do you think it should be? Would you give me courage to pursue this, so that I can grow closer to you and become a happier and healthier person?"

Faithfulness and Consistency

Accountability does not work well unless we are committed to meeting with our accountability partner faithfully on a consistent basis. If we are held accountable only once in a while, it's almost the same as not being held accountable at all! One of the things I love about my accountability brothers in my men's prayer group is that we meet every two weeks, and we are committed to make this group a priority. I will not allow myself to randomly skip a meeting for some lame reason or because I have been spiritually struggling. Accountability always helps me (even when it hurts), since it gives me the opportunity to be honest with God, myself, and at least one other person on a regular basis.

Obstacles to Accountability

A big reason that many of us shy away from accountability is pride; we hate to admit, even to ourselves, that we need help. Another reason we might shy away from accountability is because we lack real friendships. In today's world, many friendships are based upon a common activity like playing a sport; but a true friend that you can really trust can be hard to find. If pride is your issue, ask God to humble you - and then look out - because He will. And if you honestly feel that you do not have a deep friendship with someone that you can really trust, I want to encourage you to join a youth group or a prayer group, since good people like that often can be found in such groups. And if no such group is available, you might consider asking your parish priest or another trusted adult in your community to keep you accountable. Finally, if there really is no such person in your life that you think you can trust with your heart, ask God to send someone your way. Then keep your eyes and heart open, for God will be answering that prayer.

Specifically, Regarding Sexual Purity

Though there can be many dimensions to spiritual accountability, I want to focus some attention on the area of sexual purity because I believe that sexual impurity is the number one obstacle that keeps most men (and many women) in today's world from enjoying an awesome relationship with God because of the guilt and shame involved. Because of the often hidden dimension of sexual sin, very few people ever talk openly about it. Yet sexual temptation is everywhere, in the form of suggestive jokes and conversations, in tight or skimpy clothing, and in the increasingly sexualized content of the media: magazines, movies, music, television, cable, and the Internet. To highlight just one aspect of this problem, check out this statistic from a recent study:

> Forty-two percent of Internet users aged 10 to 17 surveyed have viewed online pornography in the past year. (76)

With all of this sexual temptation out there, what are we to do? Sadly, many people simply give up and choose impurity. However, I hope that you want more and are unwilling to settle for less! The road God calls us to travel is difficult. But who wants to be a wimp, caving in to every temptation that they face? Wouldn't you rather be a warrior in this battle against evil, striving for victory, and honor, and glory? I know I would!

In my opinion, there is nothing like an accountability partner to help you to restore and maintain your moral integrity and sexual purity.

Identify Your "Triggers"

As you begin the process of accountability, especially in the area of sexuality, I'd like to encourage you to consider whether there are certain times or places where temptation to impurity is more likely to occur. When I was growing up, I was asked to memorize an "Act of Contrition" to pray during Confession. One of the great lines of that excellent prayer is:

> "I firmly resolve, with the help of thy grace, to sin no more and to avoid the near occasion of sin." (77)

What is the near occasion of sin for you? Take inventory. Is there a certain person or group of people that you hang out with who influence you negatively? Are there certain channels that you have access to on cable that show sexual content? Are there DVDs in your home that cause you to lust or to have impure thoughts? Do you have a TV or computer in your room that tempts you to view inappropriate things? Is your time of temptation late at night, when everyone else is in bed? When you are babysitting at a particular home? Is it early in the morning, late at night, in the shower? Are you more lustful when you listen to certain music or certain artists?

Men - do you need to throw away your *Sports Illustrated* Swimsuit Issue or stop looking at the *Victoria's Secret* Catalogue? Are there posters of women in your room that you should take down? I encourage you to be a man and to be honest about what might lead you to be less than a real man.

Ladies - do you read romance novels that you know you shouldn't, or read articles in certain magazines that are about sexual things? Are there certain outfits that you should not wear because they are too skimpy or low-cut and therefore might lead the men in your life to lust? Do you flirt with or dance with guys in ways that lead them to think less of you than who you really are? Our world desperately needs more women of integrity; please do whatever it takes to grow in true womanhood.

You see, there are different triggers for different people. It is important to be honest about yours and to then take practical steps to protect your heart and mind so that these triggers don't cause damage to your soul.

On a personal level, I needed to confess to my accountability partners, my wife, and a priest in Confession that I found myself surfing channels late at night and watching certain shows that were not good for me. These shows were destructive to my purity because they caused me to look at women as objects and to think of sexuality as something that is merely physical; so those kinds of shows were (and still are) the near occasion of sin for me. All I can say is that it really helps me to make better choices when I know that key people in my life who really care about me might ask me about my late-night viewing habits at any time. Someone once told me that sin is like fungus in that it grows in the dark, but it starts to die when it is in the light. Accountability is one of the ways that we bring our sins into the light so that we can watch them die – and then see ourselves begin to live more fully!

Drastic Measures

In the battle for our souls, we need to desperately want God to win and the devil to lose – and sometimes that demands drastic measures. I know someone who changed to a different cable TV plan so that pornography would no longer be available – he removed that near occasion of sin. Other friends have humbly admitted their struggles with impurity to friends, asking to have their TVs or PCs programmed to block out objectionable materials, giving control of the password to their accountability partner. Teens have chosen to have their parents help them by asking to have the computer removed from their room and set up in a more public place. I know girls who have encouraged one another, as they go out on dates, to stay pure. As I became aware how important accountability is for me, I helped to establish a men's prayer group, which is my accountability group that I attend faithfully. Recently, in this accountability group, we decided to implement a zero-tolerance policy; that is, we will confess to one another if we fail in any way to live a life of moral integrity or sexual purity. What drastic measures might God be calling you to? Might He even be calling you to start an accountability group for your peers? Ask Him about that, and then listen up for His direction...

Technology Can Help

Even though technology produces many moral challenges for all of us, there are a lot of ways that technology can help us to be more accountable in living for Christ. We can send our accountability partners emails asking how they are doing. We can sign up for email lists that contain inspirational thoughts, prayers, Bible verses, or reflections on Christian spirituality. (78) I have installed free accountability software (79) on all of the PCs in my home; it regularly sends an email to accountability partners, reporting any visits to objectionable websites. Everyone in our home knows of this software, and it helps people to avoid temptation when they know someone gets a report like this emailed to them. And, to protect my children, I have installed filtering software on the PC they use which blocks out inappropriate material so that they won't accidentally surf onto inappropriate web sites. (80)

A Closing Thought - Repent and Believe

One of the most basic ways to summarize the Gospel message is through these words of Jesus:

> *This is the time of fulfillment. The kingdom of God is at hand. Repent, and believe in the gospel. (81)*

To repent means to admit our sins, confess them, ask for God's forgiveness, trust in His mercy, turn away from sin, and turn toward God. We can do this any time, not only in our personal prayer time, but also in our relationship with an accountability partner and through the sacrament of Reconciliation. (82)

To believe means to trust in, cling to, and rely on God. I encourage you to trust in God for everything, cling to Him as your best friend ever, and rely on Him as you strive to live for Him. Don't ever forget that with God all things are possible - even accountability – especially when we remember the Lone Ranger and an Indian named Tonto.

The Case of the Boiling Frog

Don't try this at home. I repeat – do not try this at home!

I once heard it said that if you take a frog, which is a cold-blooded animal, and place it in a pan of really hot water, it will jump out immediately. The frog knows that it has been placed in a dangerous environment and therefore escapes as quickly as possible. However, they say that if you take that same frog and place it in a pan of lukewarm water, that it will just sit there contentedly, feeling no danger. And, if you very gently place that pan of lukewarm water on the stove and very gradually turn up the heat, the frog's body temperature will slowly adjust to the temperature of the water it is in. The frog will continue to sit there, contently peering over the side of the pan, even as the water gets dangerously hot and the steam curls around its nostrils. Left in that situation, the frog will eventually boil to death.

I feel a need to say just one more time – don't try this at home!

The story is a parable as to what can happen in life, and I know firsthand because it totally happened to me! You see, I was that frog, and the water was my environment. When I was a young child, I believed what my parents and teachers taught me and I trusted my conscience. I made good choices, tried to be Christian, and avoided bad things like drugs and alcohol. I even remember once when I was in grade school that an older kid offered me drugs; I immediately ran home and told my parents. I jumped out of that hot water quicker than the frog. However, as I started to get older, other things began to influence me more than my parents and teachers. I began to pay more attention to other voices. I listened to more music, watched more TV and movies, read more magazines, and began to care more about what my peers thought – even though, looking back, I see now that most of them were actually very lost and confused and still trying to figure out what life was all about. The water around me began to heat up, but I was not even aware that it was happening. I started to believe a very dangerous and subtle message from these combined voices that said, "Do whatever you want to do, especially if it feels good and doesn't hurt other people too much. And don't get caught up in the guilt trip that religion gives you – all of those commandments and restrictions are pretty outdated anyway!" As I gradually distanced myself from God, people who really loved me, opportunities to grow in faith, and the strong moral values I had earlier embraced, I found myself in an environment where – like the frog – I was slowly dying. I know that you might think that I'm being dramatic, but I assure you I'm not. Had I continued in that lifestyle, I might have died; I certainly never would have experienced all of the blessings I now enjoy. Thankfully, a good friend in college helped to pluck me out of the boiling water – and I am forever grateful for his influence in helping me to rediscover God.

This concept of listening to the wrong voices and making bad choices is not just my story. It is the story of every person, and it even echoes the story of original sin, where Adam and Eve listened to the serpent instead of God. And the idea of sin leading to death is a very strong biblical principal. In the Bible it says, "The wages of sin is death..." (83) But this concept is not only biblical; it is obvious, intensely practical, and totally true. In this world that we all live in, I see people dying all of the time, and I bet you do, too. However, it's not usually physical death. The death that results from sin is spiritual, emotional, and physical. Spiritual death happens any time we make a sinful choice, because sin separates us from God who is the source of our spiritual lives. Emotional death comes because we turn to sinful behaviors instead of dealing with our complicated and deep feelings of hurt, pain, and confusion in healthy ways. And, if you live long enough, you will see that a lot of people end up physically dead because of the bad choices they make. Yes, the wages of sin is death, though it can be very subtle like it was for me and for the frog.

This is a big bummer, but it is only half of the story, and not even the most important half. I have great news for you, and it comes from God. Although "The wages of sin is death...", that same Bible verse continues with "...but the gift of God is eternal life in Christ Jesus our Lord." If you are at all interested in being free from the wages of sin and in being free to experience the gift of eternal life that God offers, then keep reading. We are going to explore the meaning of the word – freedom.

In the movie *Braveheart*, the character William Wallace said, "It's all for nothing if you don't have freedom." That line speaks volumes to my heart. "It's all for nothing if you don't have freedom."

As an American, one of the things I value the most is freedom. Many wars have been fought throughout our history, and countless millions have died defending and preserving our freedom. But what is freedom?

I'll be honest. When I was growing up, I didn't really understand what freedom is all about. Especially in my early teens, I thought that freedom meant that I could do whatever I wanted to do, whenever I wanted to do it. But that is not freedom; it is called 'free will'. And, the choices that we make with our free will, when they are inconsistent with God's plan for our lives, lead to slavery and death. Let me explain with a few examples.

Although someone might use their free will to smoke, they can become enslaved to a nicotine addiction, and even experience the slavery of premature illness and death due to diseases directly related to smoking; it happens a lot! Though someone might exercise their free will to get drunk, they can actually lose their freedom when they make really bad choices while intoxicated, choices ranging from sexual experimentation to drunk driving. Though someone may use their freedom to become sexually active, there are huge losses of freedom with STDs, unplanned pregnancies, abortion, and damaged reputations. Though someone might use the gift of free will to view pornography, the loss of freedom that results can be devastating – addiction, lust, and distorted views of human sexuality. These are just a few examples, though there are many more – cutting, eating disorders, gossip, drug abuse, etc. The crazy thing is that most people who try these things ultimately desire to become freer, but they end up losing their freedom and hurting countless other people in the process. I could tell you many more tragic stories, and I bet you could tell me some, too. But, for now, let's move on to the good news.

It is God's desire for you to experience real freedom, even if you have already lost your freedom in some way. It is not easy to be free; that is why so many people are enslaved. What I want to ask you right now is, "How badly do you want to be free?" Living a life of freedom will at times be very difficult, so I want to encourage you right now to make a personal commitment to God that you are willing to do whatever it takes to cooperate with His grace to become free. If you are ready to make that decision, pray this prayer with me right now –

Jesus, I give you permission to reveal my slaveries to me; not for a guilt trip, either – I have been on too many of those already! Show me my slaveries so that I can know what I must do to gain freedom, or to retain my freedom. I want to become the person that you created me to be – nothing less – and I am willing to do whatever it takes to become free, and to stay free. Please help me, Jesus, because I know that true freedom is possible only with your help. Thank you, Jesus. Amen.

If you want to stay free, or regain your freedom, or ever want to help someone escape their personal slaveries, I want to give you hope. Some great practical advice follows. Here it is, first of all from Jesus -

If you remain in my word, you will truly be my disciples, and you will know the truth, and the truth will set you free. (84)

What that means is that we need to be familiar with what the Bible teaches us about ourselves, reality, and life. Read the Bible. There is a whole chapter of this book devoted to reading the Bible called "Ugly Emily". In addition to the Bible, the following are several things that God has set up to help us in our pursuit of freedom:

1) Your parents. Whatever you are struggling with, I encourage you to talk to your parents. I am a parent, and so I know well that parents are far from perfect. But I also know that (with a few rare exceptions) parents love their children more than anyone else on the planet ever could. You can trust your parents to do whatever it takes to help you in your life.

2) A counselor or a therapist. If I had skin cancer, I would not be so arrogant as to try to take care of it myself; that would make me that 'special kind of stupid' person that I really don't want to be. It is the same with the bigger struggles in life; we often need the help of a trained professional. Some people have told me that counseling hasn't done much for them because they didn't 'click' with their counselor. If that is your story, I encourage you to keep trying until you find a counselor or therapist you click with!

3) Other trusted adults. There are adults in your life who really love you. Who are they? It could be your priest, youth minister, a relative, or another member of your community. For those of us pursuing freedom, we need all the help we can get! So ask God to reveal to you who the trusted adults are in your life that you should share your heart with,

and then pray for the courage to talk to them about your problems. It will really help.

4) Good friends. If you hang out with people who are pursuing lives of freedom, the positive impact will rock your world. On the other hand, friends who are enslaved can be a profoundly negative influence. I am not saying that we should ditch our friends who are struggling – that would be wrong! However, we do need moral support to live a Christian life, and this is why it is crucial to stay in regular contact with people who are good examples to us. For this reason, I am a huge fan of youth groups, teen prayer groups, and teen Bible studies. Our choice of friends will profoundly influence our future. Pray for good friends, seek out good friends; and when you find them, do all that you can to keep them in your life.

5) Twelve-step programs. Anyone struggling with serious issues should seek out a twelve-step group for the awesome support and resources that are available. Untold numbers of people have found an authentic path to freedom through the variety of twelve-step programs that are available. These programs include alcoholics anonymous, narcotics anonymous, overeaters anonymous, and many more. The principles learned in 12-step programs can help in the pursuit of freedom in any area of struggle. For help finding a 12-step group near you, ask a trusted adult or counselor.

6) Last but not least, keep praying and stay close to Jesus. He desires your freedom even more that you could. He even died to set you free. Never forget that He's got your back.

After all, who wants to be a boiling frog? Not me. I am created to be so much more than that, and I refuse to settle for less. Join me. William Wallace is right – "It's all for nothing if you don't have freedom."

The Final Chapter — Heaven

I want to live like Heaven is a real place.
--Charlie Peacock (85)

If I weep, let it be as a man who is longing for his home.
--Rich Mullins (86)

My first experience of death, at least the death of someone whom I loved deeply, happened when I was about 10 years old. My grandma died, and it blindsided me. I knew that she was sick in the hospital, but I never expected her to die.

She was such an amazing woman, and all of my memories of her are positive. She was a hugger and a kisser. She always had cookies, candy, and Kool-Aid for us grandkids; and when you are a kid, it just doesn't get any better than that! There were always fun things to do at her house; I most remember spending hours at her house doing puzzles with my sisters.

When she died, I was stunned. It hurt, very deeply, and confused me. How could someone so good be taken away from us? And then, quite unexpectedly, something happened at her funeral that I will never forget. The congregation was singing that classic church song "I am the Resurrection and the Life" and one of the lines from the song (which is also a line from Jesus in the Bible) jumped out at me and went straight to my heart: "He who believes in me will never die." At that moment I knew, with knowledge far deeper than logic and way beyond words, that my grandma was OK. She was with Jesus, and I will see her again some day. No agnostic, atheist, or skeptic will ever be able to convince me otherwise. She is in Heaven, waiting for me. End of discussion.

My grandma's death was my first experience of God. I think God knew that my fragile heart needed some love and assurance, and so God just went ahead and gave it to me supernaturally. What a gift! Thanks, God.

In this last chapter of this book, I would like you to consider death, even your own death, and what it means. In my years of working with teens I have learned that tragedy, particularly death, is a time when many people feel very close to God; it is also a time when many others feel quite distant from God. I believe that if we have faith and if we trust in God, death can bring us closer to God since death causes us to think about eternity.

I don't know about you, but I think that this world is an awesome place. I love it, and have been blessed by being able to explore some of its beauty – a quiet Ozark stream, the Rocky Mountains, the Atlantic Ocean, and the Black Hills of South Dakota. Some day I hope to visit the Grand Canyon and Yellowstone. But, as beautiful as all these might be, my heart longs for even more beauty.

I love the people I have met on this Earth. I have great friends, a wonderful family, awesome children, and an amazing wife. The teens that I've met as a youth minister continue to blow me away with their love and enthusiasm. And yet, as good as those relationships are, my heart longs for more.

I long for more because everything in this world, as good and great as it is, remains imperfect. I also long for more because as much as there is goodness on this Earth, both in nature and in relationships, there is also a lot of bad stuff, too – war, terrorism, disease, pain, hunger, loneliness, broken hearts, fear, and death. I just refuse to believe that this world is all there is. My heart tells me there must be more.

Jesus promised us that if we get to know Him better, we will experience abundant life (87) on this Earth; that has been true for me. But this world is not our home. We have been created for eternity, and our hearts cry out for relationships with others and with God that will last forever. BFF - Best Friends Forever - is not just a way that sixth grade girls sign the notes they pass back and forth in math class. It is really God's plan for us – to experience for eternity what we have been given a taste of here on Earth.

Heaven is real; and when we die, it will actually be the beginning of a newer and more full life in Heaven, a life that will be ten billion times better than this one and that will go on forever. The Bible actually describes Heaven in this way -

> On this mountain the Lord of hosts will provide for all peoples a feast of rich food and choice wines, juicy, rich food and pure, choice wines. On this mountain he will destroy the veil that veils all peoples, the web that is woven over all nations; he will destroy death forever. The Lord God will wipe away the tears from all faces; the reproach of his people he will remove from the whole earth; for the Lord has spoken. On that day it will be said: "Behold our God, to whom we looked to save us! This is the Lord for whom we looked; let us rejoice and be glad that he has saved us! (88)

I don't know about you, but to me Heaven sounds like the best Catholic wedding reception ever – great food and drink, good friends, laughing and dancing and partying that never ends! And we will have the best Host ever, One who knows and will meet all of our deepest needs and desires. Now that is a place I want to be!

I know that my grandma is there, along with my mom and so many other loved ones who have gone before me. And I plan on being there. I encourage you, with all of my heart, to live in such a way as to make it there. Does your heart long for reunion with loved ones you have lost? Does it desire to spend eternity with those you love here on Earth? That is precisely what our Lord promises.

We can attain Heaven by growing closer and closer every day with the One who wants to be our Best Friend forever. Jesus.

Sinners on Prayer
Appendix for the Chapter
"Pleasure to Angels"

Since I am a "quote guy", I just had to include in this book some of my favorite quotes on prayer. I thought about calling this appendix "Saints on Prayer", but then I decided not to - since not everyone I am going to quote is a canonized saint in the Catholic Church and because all of us (even the saints) are sinners - and I suspect that the saints are even more aware of this than the rest of us are!

I find these quotes awesome, helpful, challenging, and inspiring. I hope you do, too.

+++

How to pray? This is a simple matter. I would say: Pray any way you like, so long as you do pray.
--Pope John Paul II (89)

God is always and everywhere present to us. However, we are not always present to God. In prayer, we bring ourselves, as we are, with an openness to meet more than ourselves. We develop a way of seeing and hearing that opens us up to more than the chattering of our own thoughts and feelings.
--Fr. Joe Kempf (90)

The secret to face not only emergencies but exhaustion and personal and social problems day after day is in prayer, made in faith. Whoever prays does not get discouraged, not even in the face of the most serious difficulties, because he feels God by his side and finds refuge, serenity, and peace in his open arms.
--Pope John Paul II (91)

If we are not people of prayer, then all that we will have to offer others is ourselves.
--Sr. Eva Maria Ackermann (92)

I want at least to tell Him frequently that I love Him; this is not difficult, and it keeps the fire going.
--St. Therese of Lisieux (93)

"Jesus, I trust in you!" This is the simple prayer that Sister Faustina has taught us and which we can have on our lips in every instance of our life.
--Pope John Paul II (94)

My little children, your hearts are small, but prayer stretches them and makes them capable of loving God. Through prayer we receive a foretaste of heaven

and something of paradise comes down upon us. Prayer never leaves us without sweetness. It is honey that flows into the soul and makes all things sweet. When we pray properly, sorrows disappear like snow before the sun.
--St. John Vianney (95)

The Lord's Prayer is the most perfect of prayers...In it we ask, not only for all the things we can rightly desire, but also in the sequence that they should be desired. This prayer not only teaches us to ask for things, but also in what order we should desire them.
--St. Thomas Aquinas (96)

Try to feel the need for prayer often during the day and take the trouble to pray. Prayer makes the heart large enough until it can contain God's gift of Himself.
--Mother Teresa (97)

I strongly suspect that if we saw all the difference even the tiniest of our prayers make, and all the people those little prayers were destined to affect, and all the consequences of those prayers down through the centuries, we would be so paralyzed with awe at the power of prayer that we would be unable to get up off our knees for the rest of our lives.
--Peter Kreeft (98)

To pray well you must think of Jesus on the cross. Surely you can see how impossible it is to be distracted when you see your Brother crucified.
--Blessed Brother Andre (99)

Often a deep and fervent look at Christ is the best prayer: I look at Him and He looks at me.
--Blessed Mother Teresa (100)

When you pray, think about the blessings you have received; then at the end of the day count out on each finger the words spoken to you by Jesus: 'You did this for me.'
--Blessed Mother Teresa (101)

This final quote is not from a sinner. And yet, I thought it would be fitting to close this appendix with this thought on prayer from the ultimate Desire of all who pray -

For I know well the plans I have in mind for you, says the LORD, plans for your welfare, not for woe! Plans to give you a future full of hope. When you call me, when you go to pray to me, I will listen to you. When you look for me, you will find me. Yes, when you seek me with all your heart, you will find me with you, says the Lord.
--God (102)

The Word from Your Peers

Appendix for the Chapter "Ugly Emily"

In the chapter "Ugly Emily" I encouraged you to read the Bible, which is a completely awesome book that can totally apply to your life and deeply touch your heart. However, don't just take my word for it, take the "The Word" (get it - lol) from your peers! While writing this book, I shot out a quick email to a group of teens that I know and respect, asking them to share their favorite Bible story or passage; and here are some of the very cool things they wrote back to me to share with you...

My favorite story is David and Goliath in 1 Samuel. How cool is it that this little kid killed a giant with a sling and a stone! To me, this shows that no matter how big something is that God will never leave your side.

My favorite specific passage is Proverbs 27:17: "As iron sharpens iron, so man sharpens his fellow man." To me, this means that we impact others - so if we act as God would act, then others will. But if you act mean and selfish, you will have a bad impact on people and they will act like that.

I love Jeremiah 29:11. I remember that when I was younger and totally scared of anything bad happening to my family or me, my mom showed me this verse. It says how God has a plan and that He makes everything happen for a reason. So I started considering this and praying about it and I was actually just thinking last night how much less worrying I've done knowing God has it all worked out for me. That was a pretty big thing because I was really scared. Like my parents took me to therapy (which helped), but once I started praying more, that also helped a lot.

Of all the verses in the Bible my truly absolute favorite is Jeremiah 29:11, "For I know well the plans I have in mind for you, says the Lord, plans for your welfare, not for woe! Plans to give you a future full of hope." I like this verse because it reminds me how much God loves me and knows what is best for me. Jeremiah was just like me - a young guy called by God. He had no idea what God had planned, and no idea what he signed up for when he said "Yes." That is what makes this verse even cooler, God has a plan, and it is a plan He knows is best for me. The first few verses of Jeremiah go great with this verse. Check out Jeremiah 1:5-10, too, if you have a chance. It says how God doesn't call the qualified; Jeremiah was just a kid with a speaking impediment. God qualifies the called and He is not too picky about who He calls. Christ called a couple of fishermen and a tax collector to be his Apostles. God calls us in the same way that He called Jeremiah and the Apostles. God knew each one of us before we were born and He has a great plan for us, if only we would follow it.

My favorite quote is Habakkuk 2:3-4, "For the vision still has its time, presses on to fulfillment, and will not disappoint; If it delays, wait for it, it will surely come, it will not be late." I first read this when I was going through a really hard time trusting God...like someone once told me, the hardest and scariest thing is to realize you're in God's hands. When I read this quote I realized that God does have everything and that I can trust Him - and though I don't know my future, He does. And though I wanna know what I am doing and how I am supposed to get there, I have to realize that He will reveal to me what He wants me to know when it's time for me to know - and sometimes you just have to wait, even if it seems what you are looking for is right around the corner.

I was on a week-long retreat, and there I found my favorite verse in Ephesians 4:29 - "Let no evil talk come out of your mouths, but only what is useful for building up, as there is need, so that your words may give grace to those who hear." Basically, it's a greater call to holiness, by avoiding gossip, complaining, sarcasm, and other forms of evil talk. I admit I've never been the best at keeping this, but through this "rule", I see how destructive the power of my words can be to someone else. I also realize where I am weak when it comes to this. Throughout the week, if anyone was speaking in these ways, any other person who heard them was allowed to say "429" directly to them. It wasn't that they were necessarily criticizing or correcting them, but they did so to help the person who was speaking the slander to realize what God thinks about it. It hit me hard whenever I heard it, and definitely inspired me to become more holy. I brought this helpful reminder home and told my family, friends, and even the kid I babysit about it, and now we regularly use it, saying "429" whenever someone's speaking slander. It's a natural part of my faith life now, and every time I hear it or am called on it, I know Christ is calling me to be a stronger daughter who should avoid all the gossip, sarcasm, and complaining I so easily slip into.

Running has always been an important part of my life. My junior year of high school I was faced with a stress fracture that left me sidelined from my team. I was really struggling with the injury, and my hope of making it back for the end of my Cross Country season was quickly fading. During that time I came across some amazing words that Saint Paul writes in Romans 5 verses 3-5: "We rejoice in our suffering because we know that suffering produces endurance, endurance produces character, and character produces hope, and hope does not disappoint us because God has poured His love into our hearts through the Holy Spirit who has been given to us." After reading this, I had been given a whole new perspective on hardship. Not only would my struggle make me a better and stronger person, but the scripture assured me that God was there for me, helping me to persevere through my suffering. He wasn't just there to put His arm around me; he poured His Spirit into my heart. I felt like God was holding my heart, promising to protect it always. Surely, I am to face more difficult obstacles than a stress fracture in years to come, but knowing that God is molding me into a better person and guiding me through my suffering, I am certain I can overcome anything.

This passage from the Bible always reminds me of the Lord's steadfast love for us. Second Samuel, verses 17, 19-20, from the Contemporary English Version says "You reached down from Heaven, and you lifted me from deep in the ocean... On the day disaster struck they came and attacked me, but you defended me. When I was fenced in, you freed me and rescued me because you love me." This passage moves me because it really shows the versatility and the inexhaustible love He has for us. Whether I'm facing a challenge or defeat in the world around me or suffering in the world within me, He is there waiting for me to reach out my hand and take His.

"I am sure that nothing can separate us from God's love. Not life or death, not angels or spirits, not powers above, or powers below. Nothing can separate us from God's love for us in Jesus Christ our Lord." (Romans 8:38-39). There really is no specific story that goes with this. I found it one day in the Bible and thought about and realized that God is SO great that NOTHING (like it says) can separate me from Him. No matter where I go or how far away I drift from Him, He himself and His unending love will ALWAYS be there for me - in times of faith, and in times of doubt. Many doubting times I run across this scripture, but in my doubt I see a small hope of light that if I would just trust, God really is greater and there is nothing that can stand between us, unless I let it.

My friend Josh and I were talking on AIM, and our conversation was going pretty deep and we were talking about a lot of complicated things. At one point during our convo, Josh starting telling me how one of our friends had brought up the idea of college while they were talking. Now, I knew Josh didn't like thinking about college much, but what I didn't know was how scared he truly was about the future, about not knowing what direction life (and God) was taking him: his fear of the unknown. I wasn't really sure what to say, but then something profound happened. Something deep within me told me to open the Bible. I thought, "That's crazy, but I guess it's the Bible, so it wouldn't hurt." That something deep within me had me get up and find my Catholic Youth Bible and then told me to just drop the book and see where it lands. I continued to think this a bit bizarre, but I put the Bible on my bed and tried to flip it open. My hand slipped the first time. When I tried the second time the Bible opened cleanly to a place in Proverbs. The first thing I saw was an article in my Teen Bible with the headline: "Your Future". After I got past my awe and amazement at the significance of this title, I quickly read the article and saw what it referenced, Proverbs 3: 5-8, which talks about handing over one's trust to God and not relying on one's own intelligence, pride, etc. I thought those verses over and then decided to let Josh in on my little revelation. I typed out the Bible verses. At this point my mouth was already dropped open, but God's working doesn't stop when miracles are taking place, so once Josh read the verses he responded, "Wow u kno how fitting that is in so many ways." He then went on to decribe to me how exactly those exact Bible verses fit what was going on in his life at that exact time. It was truly a God thing. We went on to talk about how God truly works in the absolute coolest ways and again, how fitting those verses were for him. Now, Josh and I had had some "God experiences" through IM conversations before, but this was the icing on the cake!

My favorite scripture quote is from Psalm 23 "Yea though I walk through the valley of the shadow of death I will fear no evil; for thou art with me, thy rod and *thy staff they comfort me."* When I was in fifth and sixth grade, I was having a lot of problems emotionally. I thought that my life was over. I thought that I was dead spiritually, and I was harming myself physically due to my bad habits and poor decisions. I thought it was the end for me; not physically, but spiritually and emotionally. However, it wasn't. Even though I believed God had deserted me, He hadn't. I just didn't open my eyes, mind, and heart to Him; so therefore I did not notice that He was there with me and had been the whole time. Then someone came into my life and gave me a wakeup call. I realized that I could not just sit back and let myself die spiritually when there were improvements that I could make to change that. Through hard work, progress, and fallbacks, I was able to better myself physically and spiritually. I am still working on healing myself emotionally, but with God's help and my dedication I know that it can be accomplished. All I needed was that one person to come into my life and give me a wake up call. That wake up call stirred up my faith and deepened the bond I have with God. I know now that many "valley(s) of the shadow of death" will come my way, but I also know that God is here for me and His love for me can and will surpass all of my trials and tribulations.

Mark 5:21-43 (A Dead Girl and a Sick Woman) This passage means a lot to me because it has my two favorite personal Bible quotes in it: "Daughter, your faith has healed you. Go in peace and be freed from your suffering" (Mark 5:34) and "Don't be afraid; just believe" (Mark 5:36). Everyone sins - I know I have. My main problem is coming to terms with the beautiful body God put me in. I hate my body to the point that I've even attacked it with bulimia and cutting. Unfortunately, my self-hatred just grew with every act of self-destruction. But as I've grown in my faith, I've grown in love for myself. I think this is mainly because you can't fully love God until you're able to fully love everything He gives you - especially yourself. The trouble was, once I realized how amazing I am, I felt incredibly guilty about what I had done to this amazing gift. I got really depressed, and wanted to know that God forgave me, even though what I had done to myself was beyond even my own understanding. I actually didn't have a Bible, because I had given my old one to my sister. One of my friends heard this and immediately offered to give me one of hers. I started reading it and BAM - Mark 5:34 - I'm forgiven. God doesn't hate me. I think He's just happy that I can see the beauty in life again, instead of focusing on how something as small as my appearance fits into it. Unfortunately (and most other bulimics and anorexics will tell you this), an eating disorder never really leaves you. You never really feel skinny or pretty. Don't get me wrong; sometimes I look in the mirror and LOVE what I see. It's just that there's always a doubt in my mind: "This will never last...I'm too ugly to really be this pretty, it must just be the light..." Somewhere in me I know that voice is wrong. But after giving that voice so much power, it's nearly impossible to just turn it off. That's where the second verse comes into place: I'm not afraid to try and look pretty, or to think nicely about myself, because I do not believe that God made me to feel like trash. I just believe that I am beautiful, and I feel my insecurities bow before God's Own Word. The Word of God has kept me alive and is allowing me to be myself when I could so easily get pulled into self-destruction again. The Bible is not just a part of my life; it helps make life worth living.

Nothing Like Going Down a Slide...
Appendix for the Chapter
"Jon & Amber's Keg Party"

As I said in the chapter for which this is an appendix, I used to consider community service comparable to going "down a slide covered with razor blades into a swimming pool filled with acid"; but it's not nearly as painful as that, if we have the right attitude. I have actually heard countless people, including many teens, say some variation of the following words about community service: "I think I got more out of it than the people that I served". That can happen to you, too – you can get so much from serving others – when you pour your heart, your life, and your energy out for others and do something creative and valuable with the time, talents, and treasure that God has entrusted to you.

Here are the things that I have actually known young people to do, and I share them with in the hopes of sparking your own creativity.

- Volunteer every summer to help with Vacation Bible School so that younger kids can know Jesus better.
- Attend weeklong service projects (like Project Life and Christpower here in St. Louis) with your youth group to help real people with real needs.
- Raise money to go to Africa to help communities in abject poverty.
- Ask for donations to be given to victims of natural disasters instead of receiving gifts for your birthday.
- Invite those who eat lunch alone at school to join you for lunch.
- Volunteer to give retreats to your peers (through a ministry like the REAP Team, for example).
- Organize a 'root beer kegger' (complete with special t-shirts) like Jon and Amber did so that friends can party in a safe and chemical-free environment.
- Leave Ash Wednesday ashes on your forehead all day long (even at a public school) as a witness to faith and as a conversation starter.
- Start a pro-life website to alert others to the dangers of embryonic stem cell research and human cloning.
- Start a youth group at a church that doesn't have one.
- Make a decision to not talk about other people behind their backs.
- Witness peacefully to the sanctity of human life in Washington, D.C. and outside of abortion clinics.
- Sing at Mass at a Catholic school - even when no one else does.

- Enter (or simply visit) a seminary to figure out if God might be calling you to be a priest,
- Enter (or simply visit) a convent to figure out if God might be calling you to be a religious sister.
- Go on a vocation retreat with a religious community.
- Challenge a bully to stop picking on people.
- Tell a good friend about your best friend, Jesus.

This appendix, like the chapter it is for, is incomplete. If you have ideas of things that you or other teens have done that you think should be added to this appendix, send them in an email to me through this book's website (www.stirringitup.org); they just might get added either to future editions of the book or to the website itself.

More on the "F" Word
Appendix for the Chapter
"The 'F' Word"

I love the "F" word – you know, "forgiveness" (what were you thinking?) so much that I wanted to share with you some of my favorite quotes - since I am a quote guy and since these are powerful. Pick your favorite one and write it somewhere prominent – I triple dog dare you!

Forgiveness is the fragrance that the violet sheds on the heel that has crushed it.
--Mark Twain (103)

When you hold resentment toward another, you are bound to that person or condition by an emotional link that is stronger than steel. Forgiveness is the only way to dissolve that link and get free.
--Catherine Ponder (104)

There is no love without forgiveness, and there is no forgiveness without love.
--Bryant H. McGill (105)

To forgive is the highest, most beautiful form of love. In return, you will receive untold peace and happiness.
--Robert Muller (106)

To forgive is to set a prisoner free and discover that the prisoner was you.
--Lewis B. Smedes (107)

You will know that forgiveness has begun when you recall those who hurt you and feel the power to wish them well.
--Lewis B. Smedes (108)

When a deep injury is done us, we never recover until we forgive.
--Alan Paton (109)

He who is devoid of the power to forgive, is devoid of the power to love.
--Martin Luther King, Jr. (110)

Without forgiveness, there's no future.
--Bishop Desmond Tutu (111)

As the Lord has forgiven you, so must you also do.
--St. Paul (112)

Forgive us our sins for we ourselves forgive everyone in debt to us.
--Jesus, teaching us the Lord's Prayer (113)

If you forgive others their transgressions, your heavenly Father will forgive you. But if you do not forgive others, neither will your Father forgive your transgressions.
--Jesus (114)

Be merciful, just as (also) your Father is merciful. Stop judging and you will not be judged. Stop condemning and you will not be condemned. Forgive and you will be forgiven.
--Jesus (115)

Forgiveness is hard because it involves loving other people in spite of the evil that they have done to us. When we forgive, we don't deny the hurt that we have received. We don't pretend that nothing happened. But we acknowledge that there is more to the offender than the offense.
--Bishop Daniel Pilarczyk (116)

Prayer for Healing of Memories

Appendix for the Chapter
"The Worst Memory Ever"

This is a prayer that you can pray by yourself, any time. However, some people find it more beneficial to have someone pray the prayer out loud for them while they just relax and let God touch their hearts. I am willing to pray the prayer with you, if you are interested; you can download an audio version of this prayer at www.reapteam.org/healing-prayer. Just a word of warning, though – it is a long and rather relaxing prayer, and some people have been known to fall asleep during it. If that happens, know that God is with you even when you fall asleep while praying, and He is still able to deeply touch your unconscious if this happens. However, since the prayer is so relaxing, please do not listen to the audio version of the prayer while you are driving or operating heavy machinery, OK? Because, well, I hope that during the prayer you will experience God, but not necessarily face to face, if you know what I mean...

Keep in mind that this is a very thorough prayer, describing many aspects of life. And while some things in the prayer might apply to you, some may not. You can praise God for the things that don't relate to you; and if some part of this prayer really connects with a part of your life, take some time to focus your prayer on that situation. Finally, if the prayer brings up an especially big hurt that you have experienced, I would recommend talking to someone you trust for more prayer; and you might even consider counseling to ensure as much healing as possible of that particular memory. Now, let's begin the prayer. It begins with Psalm 139.

In the name of the Father, and of the Son, and of the Holy Spirit. God, I give you permission to do whatever you want to do within my heart during this prayer.

> O LORD, you have probed me, you know me:
> you know when I sit and stand; you understand my thoughts from afar.
> My travels and my rest you mark; with all my ways you are familiar.
> Even before a word is on my tongue, LORD, you know it all.
> Behind and before you encircle me and rest your hand upon me.
> Such knowledge is beyond me, far too lofty for me to reach.
> Where can I hide from your spirit? From your presence, where can I flee?
> If I ascend to the heavens, you are there; if I lie down in Sheol, you are there, too.

If I fly with the wings of dawn and alight beyond the sea,

Even there your hand will guide me, your right hand hold me fast.

If I say, "Surely darkness shall hide me, and night shall be my light" --

Darkness is not dark for you, and night shines as the day. Darkness and light are but one.

You formed my inmost being; you knit me in my mother's womb.

I praise you, so wonderfully you made me; wonderful are your works! My very self you knew;

my bones were not hidden from you, When I was being made in secret, fashioned as in the depths of the earth.

Your eyes foresaw my actions; in your book all are written down; my days were shaped, before one came to be.

How precious to me are your designs, O God; how vast the sum of them!

Probe me, God, know my heart; try me, know my concerns.

See if my way is crooked, then lead me in the ancient paths.

(117)

Lord, you know me better than I know myself. You have seen every moment of my life; from all eternity you have held me in your thoughts. You hold every moment in your heart, and have shared with me every joy, every pain. Lord, I seek healing, the healing you desire for me. I invite you to walk with me back through my past, to enable me to see my life through your eyes. I give you permission to recall to my mind anything which needs healing, knowing that you are present with me. Heal me of any pain, any guilt, any fear. I give you permission to heal me of anything: past or present, emotional or physical or spiritual - please heal me of those things that keep me from enjoying an awesome relationship with you. Help me to trust in your love. Help me to know that even the hurts and failures of my life can be transformed into channels of your grace.

Lord, walk with me back through the years of my life: through my early teen, pre-teen, and childhood years, to the time of my birth, and through those months within my mother's womb, even as far back to the very moment of my conception - that moment when you first called me into existence.

Lord, even before my mother was aware of my presence within her, when I was no larger than two cells, you knew me, you cherished me, and you loved me. Lord, even if I was considered "unwanted" or "unplanned" by my parents, help me to know that with you there are no accidents, for nothing is called into existence without your willing it to be. Thank you, Father in heaven, for giving me life.

For months I grew within the warmth of my mother's womb, close to the sound of her heart. I took shape in a marvelous way as my limbs and organs and face formed. Even in the earliest months I began to develop my personality, heard noises, and felt emotions. I could sense my mother's emotions and attitudes. Perhaps my mother was worried, fearful, or anxious. There were times when she was ill. Perhaps she was overworked and exhausted, or had a difficult pregnancy. During the pregnancy she may have experienced marriage or family problems - an abusive husband or boyfriend, other problem children, critical parents. If my mother was not married, she may have carried a sense of guilt and shame. All of these could have affected me, imprinting upon my mind and personality my own fears and guilt and emotions. Often these are the roots of some of our deepest problems. Lord, heal them. Allow your healing love to surround me and free me from any hurts I experienced in my mother's womb.

Lord, I also ask for you to heal me of any hurts associated with my birth. As the time for birth approached, I may have been fearful of leaving the security of the only surroundings I had ever known. It may have been difficult for me to move from the warmth and security of my mother's womb into a world that seemed cold, loud, and harsh. I may have experienced pain during my delivery into this world; I may even have been physically injured. There may have been complications with my delivery: perhaps I was premature; or was not breathing at first; there may have been problems with my lungs or heart; perhaps I was born handicapped. During those first moments when I needed to be held close and to be bonded with my mother and father, that may not have happened due to all the necessary medical procedures. Lord, heal any hurts associated with my birth. Let me feel the joy which you and all the angels and saints felt as I came into the world.

As a very young child, there may have arisen problems that affected me. Perhaps I never really received from my parents the love and acceptance and attention I needed. Or I may have been the "wrong" sex for my parents, who wanted a boy when I was a girl, or vice versa. Maybe sickness separated me from my mother for long periods of time. Perhaps I was cared for by someone who didn't hold me, or play with me, or help me to develop those earliest abilities necessary for my growth and learning. Daycare may have been tough for me, and I missed my parents - when they left me, I may have cried. Lord, please heal me from any hurts associated with my early childhood.

Lord, I ask you to touch and to bring healing to my relationship with my mom. Perhaps I was separated from my mother by death, or illness, or abandonment, or adoption. She may have needed to go to work and may have spent long hours away from me. There may have been other brothers and sisters who demanded much too much of her time and attention when I needed my mother to hold and feed and be with me. My mother may have harmed me in another way, by being overprotective, projecting her insecurities and fears upon me, or by not allowing me to be a little child, expecting me to grow up too quickly. Lord Jesus, heal my relationship with my mom. Help me to forgive her for her shortcomings and failings, and help me to receive from you, and from your mother, Mary, any love that was lacking in my relationship with my own mother.

Father in heaven, I also ask you to touch and heal my past and current relationship with my earthly father. There may be some hurt due to the fact that my dad was not there for me in my childhood. We may have been separated by death, divorce, abandonment, military service, or another reason. He may have been abusive, alcoholic, or unkind. Perhaps he was a workaholic who was rarely home - and when he was home, he may have paid little attention to me. Maybe he lacked the ability to relate to children, or was cold, unaffectionate, and unemotional. Father in heaven, I ask you to help me to forgive my father for the ways he was not a good father to me. Fill my heart with any lack of father's love.

Lord, I ask you to heal any hurt that I experienced due to my parents' relationship with one another. Perhaps there was tension in my parents' relationship. My memory may be full of the tension, hatred, bitterness, fighting, and abuse between my mother and father. There are those times when, though I loved them both, I felt forced to take sides. My mother may have made cutting comments about my father, or perhaps my father criticized my mother. Perhaps they separated or divorced, and my heart broke that I was unable to see them together. Perhaps there was a stepparent, or stepbrothers and sisters in my family, and these may have been painful relationships. Lord Jesus, help me to turn to you to receive what was lacking in the love between my parents. Help me to realize that they, too, were hurting, imperfect human beings. Enable me to forgive them their failings and to receive through you and your mother, Mary, the love they wanted to give me.

Brothers and sisters are a gift from you, Lord, yet they can also be the source of a lot of pain. Or perhaps I was an only child, lacking the support and love of siblings; perhaps I was one of many and lacked the personal attention I needed. There may have been times in our family when the brothers and sisters competed for our parents' love and attention, and that feeling of competition still affects our relationship. At times my parents compared my brothers and sisters with me, and I may have felt that I was not as smart, or as good looking, or as well behaved. There may have been another child who was handicapped or sickly, who received so much love and attention from my parents, and perhaps I felt jealous of this attention. Or maybe there was the brother or sister whom I wanted to be close to, who didn't return my love. Lord, forgive me for the ways I have hurt my brothers and sisters, and help me to forgive them. Heal our relationships, that we may love one another.

Many things happened as I grew in my childhood. Many good things I still remember and some I have forgotten. There are also many hurts I remember, and many are buried in my subconscious. I remember some of the times my father or mother disciplined me, perhaps too harshly for such a little child. They may have even abused me physically or emotionally. Perhaps there was sexual abuse by a family member, another person I trusted, a neighbor, or a stranger, which left me feeling frightened and shameful and used. There were times when I was afraid of the dark, or of animals, or of water or of being lost or left alone. There may have been traumatic experiences - the death of someone close, an accident, a fire or earthquake or storm, hospitalization. Perhaps I was a lonely or shy child who never felt as though I fit in and who never had many friends. Or perhaps we were poor and lacked material needs. Perhaps, because of our family's attitude, I was never introduced to you at a young age, Lord; and because of that, sometimes it is hard to believe in you now. In school, there were new friends and challenges. And there were also times when I felt like a failure. The other children could be cruel with their teasing - the nicknames that they called me hurt my feelings; and when they excluded me, I felt unimportant. There were teachers who were insensitive, who embarrassed me in front of others, disciplined me unfairly, who had too high expectations, or who were unable to help me when I had special problems.

At times I had poor grades or was unable to compete athletically. Lord, heal all my hurts from childhood. Help me to forgive those who hurt me. Make up for my failures, and for the failures of others, with your healing love.

Lord, I also want to ask you to touch and heal the hurts that I have experienced in my teenage years. Some of the hurts were long ago, some have been very recent, and some I am still experiencing at this very moment. Lord Jesus, I call upon you to begin to heal the hurts of my teen years. Quite honestly, Jesus, being a teenager has been a lot of fun. However, being a teen has also been very difficult. At times I have experienced feeling awkward, ugly, stupid, stressed out, confused, and sometimes I have even felt very alone. My emotions sometimes get jumbled between excitement and despair, joy and loneliness. Lord, help me to forgive those people who have stabbed me in the back by gossiping and spreading rumors about me. I want to forgive the people who have labeled me unfairly, who have called me names, as well as those who have ignored me and never given me a chance. Lord, I ask you to forgive me, too, because I have been guilty of the same things. I have gossiped, told lies about others, turned my back on my friends, and not given some people a chance. Forgive me, Lord, for the masks that I have worn - there are so many times that I have tried to be someone that I am not, just because I wanted to be accepted. Perhaps there are hurts associated with the dating that I have done, or maybe I feel hurt because I have been on so few dates. There have been those members of the opposite sex who ignored me for no reason, or who dumped me with no explanation, or whom I have treated unfairly. Lord, heal any hurts associated with my dating relationships, and help me to receive from you the love that my heart longs for.

Lord, there are also things that I have done that very few people know about - maybe even no one else knows about these things but you; things like sneaking out of the house, telling lies, using drugs or alcohol. There may have been rebellion against my parents or the law in an effort to express my anger. Maybe I have misused the gift of my sexuality. Perhaps there was a pregnancy or an abortion, and I may have suffered guilt. I might have a great sense of loss in my life, possibly from the loss of my virginity, or maybe even from the loss of a child. Maybe there has been involvement with pornography, or there has been homosexual activity, or maybe a venereal disease. Lord, heal my heart of any sense of loss associated with my sexuality. Forgive me Lord, and help me to forgive those who have hurt me.

And, Lord, there have been other hurts and problems in my life. There have been loved ones who have left me or who have died – in accidents, from illness, due to old age, or even suicide - leaving me feeling lonely and abandoned. I commit those people that I miss so much to your care; help me to forgive them for leaving me. Perhaps there has been trauma of some sort - serious illness, or assault, rape or robbery, or an accident. Perhaps a loved one or I have been left physically or emotionally injured, changing my entire future. Maybe I have suffered an emotional breakdown, finding myself unable to cope with all that life sends me.

Lord, sometimes I have found myself angry with you, though I might be afraid to admit it. You've seemed so far away; and when I prayed, there seemed to be no answer. Those who represented you and your Church, the priests and sisters and deacons and teachers, sometimes were insensitive and unkind. And in those moments of greatest pain, when only you could have done something – it sure feels like you didn't. Touch my anger, my hurt, and my disappointment toward you, Lord, and allow me to release it, knowing that you return only understanding and love. I forgive you, Lord God. Please forgive me for my attitudes and for my lack of intimacy toward you.

Lord Jesus, thank you for touching and healing the hurts in my life. Give me courage to seek out professional help and further prayer from trusted adults for those very big hurts I have experienced. Continue to touch and heal and love me, Jesus, for the rest of my life. I ask all of this, and I thank you for all that you have done, for all that you have begun to do, and for all that you will continue to do in my life. I give you praise, Jesus. Amen. (118)

++++++++++++++++++++

I want to share with you two quick thoughts about this prayer, now that you have prayed it. First of all, I encourage you to pray it often. Just as it is a good thing to clean your room periodically, this prayer can clean up our souls, which can get dirty with the passage of time. Second, don't be surprised if you feel the effects of this prayer at random times; you may just occasionally recall a time when you were hurt by someone, maybe even a time in the distant past. If and when that happens, simply invite Jesus into that memory, as you learned to do in the chapter "The Worst Memory Ever"; and let Him speak to that situation and help you to forgive whoever hurt you. Healing of memories is an ongoing and lifelong process...

End Notes

1. "Letter to Sheldon Vanauken" of 22nd April, 1953, quoted in *A Severe Mercy*, p. 134.
2. To find out about the REAP Team, go to www.reapteam.org
3. 2 Tim 1:6-7
4. My paraphrase of 2 Tim 1:6-7, with apologies to Biblical scholars everywhere
5. *Temptation and Discernment* by Segundo Galilea, page 47
6. Matthew 4:1-11
7. Hebrews 4:15
8. http://www.catholicschooldenton.org/Virtues.htm
9. from http://www.practicegodspresence.com/
10. Luke 11:1
11. Luke 11:2-4
12. Here are just a few resources, though there are many more - http://www.catholic.org/clife/prayers/, http://www.sacredspace.ie/, http://www.americancatholic.org/ (has a minute meditation), and http://www.universalis.com/cgi-bin/display/index.htm (which will guide you through praying the Divine Office).
13. from the album *Little Red Riding Hood*, available at www.thelostdogs.com
14. In the book *Hunting for God, Fishing for the Lord* by Fr. Joseph Classen, page 95
15. *Counsels and Reminiscences* by St. Therese, http://www.catholicplanet.com/ebooks/Counsels-and-Reminiscences.pdf.
16. http://www.monksofadoration.org/op03.html
17. You can hear an entire interview with Sister Carol on the REAP Team website; it is one of our podcasts and you can find it at http://www.reapteam.org/sister-carol-interview
18. Psalm 46:10
19. To read the original, see St. Augustine's *Confessions*, Book Eight, Chapter XII, Paragraph 28 at http://www.sullivan-county.com/id3/confessions/augcon8.htm
20. If you want to go right now, here is the link - http://www.scborromeo.org/ccc.htm
21. This dialogue is between St. Joan and her prosecuting attorney in George Bernard Shaw's play *St. Joan*. I admit it is not a verbatim quote of St. Joan, but it captures the essence of what she believed.
22. If you want to really learn a lot about this concept of discernment, I encourage you to study the *Spiritual Exercises* of St. Ignatius of Loyola.
23. From the book *A Simple Path* by Mother Teresa
24. John 10:27
25. Genesis 1:26-27
26. Go to http://www.usccb.org/nab/bible/ or http://www.vatican.va/archive/ENG0839/_INDEX.HTM for online versions of the Bible
27. As quoted in the *Catechism of the Catholic Church* (www.scborromeo.org/ccc.htm), section 113 in the portion devoted to "Sacred Scripture in the Life of the Church" – a 'must read' section of the Catechism, in my humble opinion.
28. http://www.rc.net/marquette/carmelite/ponder_these.htm
29. I wish I could give credit to whoever came up with that quote!

30. One I really like is called *God's Word Today* which you can find at www. godswordtoday.com, but there are many other great ones, too.

31. Go to http://www.usccb.org/nab/bible/ or http://www.vatican.va/archive/ ENG0839/_INDEX.HTM for online versions of the Bible

32. Phillippians 4:13

33. John 16:33

34. If this interests you, just Google for "bible in a year" and you will find cool options.

35. Matthew 27:5

36. Luke 10:37

37. For Catholic teens, I highly recommend this dude called "The Bible Geek". He writes a regular column for lifeteen.com which you can subscribe to at that site, and he has written some great books, too. His other name, besides The Bible Geek, is Mark Hart.

38. Malachy McCourt, see http://www.brainyquote.com/quotes/quotes/m/ malachymcc307621.html

39. Do a Google image search for Mehmet Ali Agca and you will easily find the famous photo.

40. http://en.wikipedia.org/wiki/Pope_John_Paul_II#Assassination_attempts

41. From the song "To Forgive" by Steve Taylor from the album *On the Fritz*, released in 1985

42. Luke 1:37

43. Luke 23:34

44. I want to thank my daughter Audrey for this awesome analogy, which God gave her on the first talk she ever gave to a group of adults in March 2007.

45. http://www.scborromeo.org/ccc/para/1374.htm

46. If I knew who said it, I would certainly give them credit!

47. I slightly edited, for the sake of clarity, the analogy as found online at http:// members.aol.com/bjw1106/euchmir.htm

48. John 6:51-55

49. Matthew 26:26-28

50. Thanks for reminding me of this, Fr. John Leykam!

51. Thanks, Ann Clegg, for that awesome testimony on the Eucharist at that 2nd grade retreat in Normandy!

52. Check out *Jesus is the Bridegroom of His People*, a general audience of Pope John Paul II given on December 11, 1991, available at http://www.vatican.va/ holy_father/john_paul_ii/audiences/alpha/data/aud19911211en.html

53. From the song "Amateur Lovers" by the band Switchfoot on the CD *Oh Gravity!*

54. Romans 3:23

55. http://www.scborromeo.org/ccc/para/2042.htm

56. John 20:23

57. 1 John 1:9

58. http://www.catholic.com/library/Confession.asp

59. Matthew 28:20

60. Thanks for always saying that on all those REAP retreats, Danny Liston!

61. http://www.catholic-forum.com/saints/saintj14.htm

62. Matthew 18:20

63. Matthew 19:26

64. The one I would most highly recommend, since I am most familiar with it, is www.lifeteen.com, but I also have discovered www.jesusyouth.org and www.youthapostles.com.

65. Danny Liston is an excellent musician. Search the web, and buy his music...you won't regret it.

66. Though it is true that we ultimately cannot stop someone from hurting himself or herself if they really want to, it is also true that we can help people who are tempted to hurt themselves, and so I really encourage you to know the warning signs of suicide by going to http://www.crisiscenter.com/dsuicd.htm or doing a Google search for "suicide warning signs" – just in case you are ever at a place to help someone in crisis. At this point in my conversation with this young woman, however, she most needed healing, mercy, and compassion.

67. Hebrews 13:8

68. Revelation 21:5

69. To read the poem, go to http://www.footprints-inthe-sand.com/ and click on "Poem" on the left hand side of the page.

70. http://www.thenarniaacademy.org/dictionary.htm

71. http://www.livingcatholicism.com/archives/2005/04/simple_ways_to.html

72. *Letters of C.S. Lewis* (2 February 1955), p. 261

73. Quoted in *ZENIT* (Zenit.org) June 23, 2005

74. http://www.catholic.com/thisrock/2003/0309fea1.asp

75. http://www.catholic-forum.com/saints/saintt02.htm

76. http://www.msnbc.msn.com/id/16981028/

77. http://www.ewtn.com/library/PRAYER/ACTOFCON.TXT

78. Some options, of many, are *The Daily E-Pistle* at http://www.catholic-forum.com/e-pistle.html, email reflections from the daily Catholic Mass at http://gogoodnews.net/DailyReflections/index.html, and *Spread the Word* by The Bible Geek (Mark Hart) at www.lifeteen.com

79. This free software is called x3watch and can be found at www.xxxchurch.com

80. I use Cybersitter, but there are other great filtering programs, including Net Nanny and Cyberpatrol. There is a cost, but it is a small price to pay for protecting my family.

81. (Mark 1:15).

82. Read the chapter of this book called "I Reckon So" for a thorough treatment of this sacrament.

83. Romans 6:23

84. John 8:32-33

85. From the song "Heaven is a Real Place" on the CD *The Secret of Time* by Charlie Peacock

86. From the song "If I Stand" on the CD *Winds of Heaven...Stuff of Earth* by Rich Mullins

87. John 10:10

88. Isaiah 25: 6-9

89. *The Way of Prayer* by Pope John Paul II, Crossroad Publishing Co. (1995).

90. *No One Cries the Wrong Way* by Fr. Joseph Kempf, Harcourt Religious Publishers, p. 23

91. http://www.zenit.org/english/angelus_eng/visualizza.phtml?sid=24829

92. Spoken on a retreat to REAP Team members, January 3, 2004

93. http://www.ewtn.com/therese/letters/Letters6.htm

94. http://www.zenit.org/english/audience/visualizza.phtml?sid=24334

95. http://www.catholic-forum.com/SAINTS/saintj18.htm

96. http://www.vatican.net/archive/catechism/p4s2a1.htm

97. http://home.comcast.net/~motherteresasite/prayers.html

98. http://www.missionmoment.org/allmissionmoments.htm (see 1/30/06)

99. *Modern Heroes of the Church* by Leo Knowles, p. 83

100. *No Greater Love* by Mother Teresa of Calcutta, p. 7

101. http://www.st.ignatius.net/04-29-07.html

102. Jeremiah 29:11-14

103. http://www.brainyquote.com/quotes/quotes/m/marktwain109919.html

104. http://en.thinkexist.com/quotations/forgiveness

105. http://en.thinkexist.com/quotations/forgiveness

106. http://en.thinkexist.com/quotations/forgiveness

107. http://en.thinkexist.com/quotations/forgiveness

108. http://en.thinkexist.com/quotations/forgiveness

109. http://en.thinkexist.com/quotations/forgiveness

110. http://en.thinkexist.com/quotations/forgiveness

111. http://en.thinkexist.com/quotations/forgiveness

112. Colossians 3:13

113. Luke 11:4

114. Matthew 6:14-15

115. Luke 6:36-37

116. http://www.stjohnneumannchurch.org/worship/wor_pastor.html

117. Psalm 139, verses 1-18 and 23-24

118. This prayer was adapted from the "Healing of Memories Prayer" published in the *Born of the Spirit Seminar Leader's & Sponsor's Manual* written by Ron Ryan, copyright 1988 by Western Washington Catholic Charismatic Renewal. Address: WWCCR, P.O. Box 33609, Seattle, WA 98133, website: www.wwccr.org

As an added feature to this book, I have included a free audio CD!

On this CD, you'll be able to hear some pretty sweet stuff, like

I Want to Cut Off My Arm
My Stupid Fake Happy Self
Redefining Cool
Deer Hunting with God
Pope John Paul II (talking to teenagers)
and more...

Please know that you have my permission to burn unlimited copies of this CD to share with others. All I ask is that you title the CD *Stirring It Up More*, write www.stirringitup.org on it, and that you reproduce it in its entirety.

I hope you enjoy listening to it!

Peace,
Paul Masek

P.S. If for some random reason the CD is missing from this book, I can send you one. Just mail me your address and check or money order for $5.00 (because while the CD is free, there are shipping and handling costs). Make your check payable to *Out of the Box Records* and send to:

Paul Masek
Re: *Stirring It Up More* CD
27 Grand Circle Drive
Maryland Heights, MO 63043